Discovering Our Lawyer Poets

James R. Elkins

Lawlit Press
Morgantown, West Virginia

Lawlit Press
Morgantown, West Virginia

Discovering Our Lawyer Poets
© 2024 James R. Elkins
ISBN: 979-8-218-35238-7

Library of Congress Control Number: 2024901578

Cover art: *Study: the left hand of a young man holding a stick and resting on a book*, artist unknown, late eighteenth century, held at Cooper Hewitt, Smithsonian Design Museum. Public domain.

February 2025: additional dates and a small number of new entries added to the index of lawyer poets in the appendix.

Production services:
Populore Publishing Company
Morgantown, West Virginia

Contents

Acknowledgments   v

I   a journey gets underway   1
II   identifying our lawyer poets   23
III   seemingly different universes—law & poetry   51
IV   talking to lawyers about their poetry   65
V   reading the poetry of lawyers with students   85

Epilogue: twenty-two propositions   115

Appendix: a chronological index of lawyer poets (c. 1600–1950)   119

Acknowledgments

This account of my discovery of lawyer poets and their poetry—my reading of their poetry—publishing poetry—teaching the poetry—is drawn primarily from previously published works that include: an introduction to *Off the Record: An Anthology of Poetry by Lawyers*, 38 Legal Stud. F. 1–19 (2004); *In Search of the Lawyer Poets*, 11 (1) Rattle 117–124 (2005) (Tribute to Lawyer Poets, Issue #23); "Compilation of the Anthology," *in* James R. Elkins (ed.), *Lawyer Poets and That World We Call Law: An Anthology of Poems about the Practice of Law* 218–222 (Pleasure Boat Studio, 2013); "Each Year of Law School—Read a Collection of Poems," in James R. Elkins, *The Law School Journey: A Calendar of Readings* 201–205 (Carolina Academic Press, 2020). The full account of my introduction to John William Corrington's work that set my discovery of lawyer poets into motion appears in James R. Elkins, *A Great Gift: Reading John William Corrington*, 26 Legal Stud. F. 425–489 (2002).

I

a journey gets underway

NO STRANGER TO TEACHING EXOTIC COURSES, I knew I had ventured to the edge of the law school universe when I found myself teaching Lawyers, Poets & Poetry. Let me assure you, the idea for teaching the course did not emanate from an evening in the company of Kentucky bourbon. The story of the Lawyers, Poets & Poetry course takes its own meandering path . . .

■

It was a day lodged in mid-summer. Idleness and industry had settled into a quiet truce. I am, or so I tell myself, working on a manuscript about my backroads travel in the law school world, an elusive writing project, abandoned and resumed so often the pattern had become familiar. The manuscript—*Cautionary Tales: A Backroads Tour of the Law School World*—seems always just one-more-summer away from completion. On this sun-drenched summer morning, I attribute my halting effort to work on the manuscript to patience, knowing that patience can easily be confused for idleness. I reassure myself: There will be a day when a strong wind makes for the kind of sailing that wills you to finish the *Cautionary Tales* manuscript. The wind picks up this summer day but I end up sailing to a far different place—on an entirely different journey—than anything I would have imagined.

On that summer morning I had a sense—call it detached bemusement—that the confident part of me that could write had walked off stage in protest. I wouldn't dignify the stalled writing to call it writer's block. Whatever the cause of the halted writing, the postman arrives with the morning mail and a perfectly good excuse for setting aside work on the *Cautionary Tales* manuscript. The manuscript will wait. Of course I've been telling myself this for years.

On most days, the postman—bonded agent of the outside world—arrives to deliver utility bills, advertisements, and still another "final notice" from the AARP to inform me the organization deems my membership of vital importance. I depend on the postman to make his routine delivery of the day's allotment of detritus and debris—the disposable and the useless—along with a never-ending stream of bills to be paid.

On this morning, the postman delivers a rationale for putting aside the *Cautionary Tales* manuscript—a colleague's essay submitted for publication in the *Legal Studies Forum*. I took over editorship of the journal in 1996, and edited the journal for twenty-four years (*LSF* ceased publication in 2020). My involvement with the *Legal Studies Forum* goes back to the late 1970s and my first years in teaching. My years with *LSF* is another story, a story I will not attempt to tell here.

The postman, on a good day, delivers an article or an essay that must be read and evaluated, and a determination made about publication in *LSF*. The journal provides a perennial source of diversions that allow me, in good conscience, to set aside my own writing for the time required for *LSF* editing work. An editor lives a life of diversions.

I read the essay the postman delivers this summer morning with an editor's battered hope—hope scarred by a history of disappointment.[1] The essay that arrives in this morning's mail—welcome diversion that it is—turns out to be about a writer and onetime lawyer named John William Corrington and his novella, "Decoration Day," that centers on a retired judge.[2] I don't know anything about Corrington; I have never heard of him. The author of the essay, in his introduction, finds Corrington's "Decoration Day" of interest for its literary representation of Plato's search for order in the soul. Reading this, my eyes glaze over; I suspect that an explication of Corrington's novella through a Plato perspective may not be the kind of diversion that will readily support a decision to set aside what I have in mind for a day's work on the *Cautionary Tales* manuscript.

I suspect a scholarly explanation of Corrington's literary portrayal of Plato's philosophy in a work of fiction will not get me through the morning. Even so, I know I must read on and see the essay on Corrington's novella to its end—the editor under the archetypal sway of Sisyphus. Before the numb thought of composing a rejection takes hold, I read on to find, tucked away in a footnote in the essay, a brief bio of John William Corrington:

> John William Corrington received a Ph.D. from the University of Sussex in 1964 and taught English at Louisiana State and Loyola until 1973. He received his J.D. from Tulane in 1976. While practicing law in New Orleans, he remained active as a writer,

working on film and television scripts, and continued to publish novels, poetry, and short stories. Among his most significant works are the novels *The Bombardier* (1970) and *Shad Sentell* (1984), the poetry volume *Lines to the South and Other Poems* (1965), and a volume of short stories, *The Actes and Monuments* (1978).

The Corrington bio captures my attention—rouses me from languor—puts the day in a different light: *Who is John William Corrington?*

Teaching Lawyers and Literature for several decades, dutifully following the scholarly writings on "law and literature," I don't recall ever seeing a reference to Corrington or his literary work. With the prominence of lawyer novelists, learning of still another lawyer who has made the turn to fiction would not stir me to lofty thoughts. What first intrigues me about Corrington is not that he was a lawyer who wrote novels; he is a literary man who becomes a lawyer. I reread the Corrington bio. I read it again. Again. On each reading, I find Corrington more intriguing: He is an English professor. He has a Ph.D. from a university in England. He is a Hollywood screenwriter. A published poet. He ends up practicing law in New Orleans. My question: How does a poet and novelist, a professor of English Literature in the Deep South, find his way to law school and the practice of law? Other questions line up for attention: What would a man like Corrington with his background in the literary world have to say about his experience in law school? About the practice of law? About the emergence of the "law and literature" movement that emerges during the time Corrington becomes a lawyer and begins to place lawyer characters in his fiction? The

Corrington bio leaves me with the sense that Corrington is a man who might have a story or two to tell.³ Finally, the most puzzling part of the Corrington bio, what I find most difficult to get my mind around: *Corrington is a poet and a lawyer.*

Steeped in social conventions, we tend to think that lawyers and poets exist in different universes of thought and feeling, sentiment and sensibility. For lawyers, and for poets, there must be some reflection of reality embodied in the understanding that the law leads north, poetry takes you south. When you take the road north, you are most definitely not headed south. North and south take you in opposite directions. Drawing on our conventional repertoire of images—*lawyer*—*poet*—imagining a single person embodying and representing both images and ways of being can be difficult. With my introduction to Corrington, a poet who became a lawyer, I find my old working stereotypes—*lawyer*—*poet*—called into question. With my conventional thinking—about lawyers—about poets—undermined, I am curious: How does Corrington, a published poet, end up in the practice of law? Does the practice of law—being a lawyer—find a way into his poetry? What does it mean to be a *lawyer* and a *poet*?

■

Reading the John William Corrington bio, I am curious about this man. Less interested in Plato than I am Corrington, I seek out Corrington's novella "Decoration Day." ("Decoration Day" was collected with a second novella, "The Risi's Wife," in a book Corrington titled *All My Trials* (1987)). I learn the book is out of print and the university library does not have the book. I turn to abebooks.com where, wondrously, a curious man (with dollars in his pocket) can peruse the holdings of thousands of independent book dealers located around the world. A few minutes on abebooks.com and a marvelous used-book search-engine, and it's possible to locate even the most obscure book and a bookseller who will see it to your door.

July 1, 2000. I locate a paperback copy of *All My Trials* at Pinchpenny Books in Ashland, Kentucky (and how remarkable is it that *All My Trials* could have ended up in such a place; a story there I suspect, albeit one never to be told). With payment of $4.00 and $1.58 shipping, *All My Trials* is on its way.[4] In the days I wait for my copy of *All My Trials* to arrive, I learn that Corrington, collaborating with his wife, Joyce—a professor of chemistry at Xavier University, wrote the screenplay for *The Battle for the Planet of the Apes*; the screenplay was written during Corrington's first year of law school. Corrington, forty-three when he finished law school, takes up the practice of law in New Orleans. Three years into his practice, he abandons the legal profession to write TV soap operas, collaborate with his wife on detective mysteries, and write some of the most compelling fiction featuring lawyer protagonists of any writer in the twentieth century.[5]

In that now memorable distant summer, I recall waiting with eager anticipation the arrival of Corrington's *All My Trials*. I read the Corrington novella "Decoration Day." I read the accompanying second novella in *All My Trials*—"The Risi's Wife." I read the legal fiction that Corrington begins to write while he is in law school.[6] I read Corrington's short stories and his novels. I eventually read his poetry. I read everything Corrington published, and then, having worked my way through Corrington's published work, unsettled at the thought my sojourn with Corrington might be coming to an end, I found a way to continue reading Corrington. I obtain Joyce Corrington's permission to see what could be found in Corrington's unpublished work archived at Centenary College in Shreveport, Louisiana, where Corrington attended college for his undergraduate studies. Everything I read by Corrington (published and unpublished) suggests that he was an astounding writer who told stories in his fiction that few writers could equal. I had stumbled onto a writer who was, to my amazement, virtually unknown in "law and literature" circles.[7] Reading Corrington, I continue to ask myself: What drives a man to abandon the teaching of literature to become a lawyer? What might Corrington—steeped in the world of literature—a poet having made his foray into the practice of law—tell us about his time in the world of lawyers? What would lead Corrington to abandon the practice of law? Reading Corrington, watching summer fade into fall, intrigued by Corrington's lyrical writing and vivid storytelling, I now find winds conducive for sailing, but where this wind from the reading of Corrington might take me—summer coming to an inevitable end—I have no idea.[8]

■

What I find most intriguing in the Corrington biography: *Corrington is a poet. A poet who becomes a lawyer.* My first reaction, common I suspect, is that lawyers and poets exist in different universes. Poets and lawyers seem to live, or so we tend to think, in different worlds. To live a life practicing law and a life composing poetry are different kinds of lives. Lawyers and poets, from what we know of them—following the thinking laid out for us in stereotypes—are quite different kinds of creatures.

Contemplating this hybrid, poet lawyer—lawyer poet, I am intrigued and puzzled: Poetry and law are acquired tastes. They suggest different sensibilities, different ways of thinking, different ways of engaging the world. (With lawyers and poets, have we not found lived embodiments of different pursuits that arise from left-brain- and right-brain-hemisphere influence?)

That Corrington was a poet *and* a lawyer calls into question conventional stereotypes. The more I think about John William Corrington and his dual citizenship in the two worlds—poetry and law—the more I begin to see the lawyer poet as an iconoclast, a destroyer of images that have concretized into stereotypes.

Lawyer stereotypes are prevalent in the law school world. No one is more anxious about examining rigid, deep-lying lawyer stereotypes than those who have set out to be lawyers. Here is the paradox: Students who accept and adopt a common *lawyer* image—stereotype-informed—are often anxious about the narrow cast of mind they see being demanded of them, the kind of mind that fits the traditional lawyer image. Law students want to move into that glittering world of law where they can live their *lawyer* image, an image cherished and feared. Students, eager to take up a life in law, find themselves in a situation they may or may not be willing (or capable) of acknowledging: The life they seek holds great promise, a promise mortgaged with those parts of the self they must forsake—or think they must forsake—as they set forth on the long journey that lies ahead.

Some of us find we need more than law to live the life we imagine we will live; some of us have more than one archetype shaping this imagined life. John William Corrington—poet, novelist, English professor, philosopher, lawyer, screenwriter—prompts us to acknowledge, in the striking array of his talents and pursuits, that some lawyers have a life—a mind—that cannot be fully expressed in the confined endeavors of practice we associate with lawyer work.[9] William O. Douglas, the Supreme Court Justice I first admired as a student—a man of the West, traveler, writer—lived a rich life beyond the law.[10] Douglas was an iconoclast. In law, we sometimes find men like William O. Douglas and John William Corrington. I am reminded of Charles Black—constitutional law scholar, law teacher, jazz musician, and yes, a poet.[11] I fondly remember one of my own teachers, John Batt, the most engaging teacher I would ever encounter, a teacher whose imprint on my life has been unmistakable. Batt was a teacher original in his teaching (and in his writing)[12]; original in a way that made it evident he had not allowed himself to be consumed by law. No one would find it possible to think Batt had been domesticated in the way so common to teachers. Underlying Batt's teaching was the idea that we—students—could never be certain what we might need to know to be the lawyer we imagined we would become. We would need to be *smart*. Being smart required knowing beyond the law every bit as much as it required knowing the law. John Batt, in the years we remained friends and colleagues, never spoke about poets and poetry, but I am dead certain he would find intriguing, as I do, how lawyer poets take on a way of being that makes it possible for them to live in two sovereign domains: *law* and *poetry*.

Chapter I
Endnotes

1. The editors of *Crazyhorse*, a literary journal, put this matter of an editor's hope this way: "Editing a journal calls for a kind of hope steeped in stone cold reality." When the reality of what is found in the submissions to a journal's editor sets in, there is a temptation "to let our hope erode just a bit, one grain of sand worn away from the canyon walls through which flows the river of words we receive." But for *Crazyhorse* editors, hope prevails: "We continue to hope, because there are always, always moments of gold in that river, moments when words form, in the kind of mysterious alchemy good writing truly is, the treasure a fine poem or story or essay can be." "Editor's Note," *Crazyhorse*, #81 (Spring 2012).

2. My discovery of our lawyer poets has an identifiable starting place, my introduction to John William Corrington's work, thanks to Douglas Mitchell's essay *John William Corrington's* Decoration Day, 25 Legal Stud. F. 687 (2000). The Mitchell essay first alerted me to Corrington's writings, in particular "Decoration Day," a novella, along with a second novella, "The Risi's Wife," collected in John William Corrington, *All My Trials* (University of Arkansas Press, 1987).

3. For readers interested in John William Corrington's life and the stories I attempted to tell about his life, *see* James R. Elkins, *A Great Gift: Reading John William Corrington*, 26 Legal Stud. F. 425 (2002).

4   *All My Trials* is not a rare book, but it is by no means in plentiful supply. A search on abebooks.com on January 1, 2002, listed only two copies available for sale, one of them a hardcover edition offered by Turgid Tomes, a bookstore in Nashville, Tennessee, at $38 (plus shipping). Book dealers sometimes describe *All My Trials* as an "uncommon book." On May 20, 2023, abebooks.com had five copies of the book listed, two of them, in fine condition with dust jackets for less than $20. Amazon.com lists a single copy priced at $89.

5   The following biographical commentary on John William Corrington appeared on a website I created to focus on lawyer poets—Strangers to Us All: Lawyers and Poetry. A version of this bio appears in James R. Elkins, *John William Corrington*, 27 Legal Stud. F. 493 (2003). My thanks to Joyce Corrington, Bill Corrington's wife, for her efforts in seeing that I got the bio right.

John William Corrington

John William Corrington was born in Ohio in 1932; his family moved to Shreveport, Louisiana, when he was a young boy. It was Louisiana, more particularly, Shreveport, that Corrington adopted as his spiritual and literary home. Growing up in Shreveport, he developed a great love for the city and for the South, a love that figures prominently in his life and his writings. Corrington remained in Shreveport during his college years to attend Centenary College where he met a small group of teachers who he revered and honored throughout his life.

Corrington received a B.A. degree from Centenary College in 1956 and his M.A. from Rice University in 1960, the year he took on his first teaching position in the English Department at Louisiana State University. On leave from LSU, Corrington obtained his D.Phil. in 1965 from the University of Sussex (England) and then, in 1966, moved to Loyola University–New Orleans where he was an Associate Professor of English, and later chair of the English Department. Corrington's early writing included poetry, novels, short stories, and academic writing that might be labeled literary criticism. He would later write crime/detective fiction and screenplays in collaboration with his wife, Joyce Corrington.

At age forty, Corrington decided to study law. He obtained his J.D. from Tulane Law School in 1975. (Corrington's father studied law, but stayed with his insurance business and did not practice law.) After graduating from Tulane Law School, Corrington practiced law in New Orleans for three years. The influence of his legal training and law practice soon found a place in his fiction. Corrington's "legal fiction" would include six short stories (I published a newly discovered seventh Corrington story, "The Absolute Vices," in *LSF* in 2002.) The two lawyer-themed novellas published under the title *All My Trials* by the University of Arkansas Press in 1987 appeared the year before Corrington's death in 1988.

Corrington gave up the practice of law after three years to pursue TV, literary and intellectual history writing projects. He died in Malibu, California. Joyce Corrington, his wife, coauthor and collaborator, survives him and now makes her home in New Orleans.

During the 1960s, Corrington taught English literature, wrote poetry, published academic papers, and wrote his first novels. His first poetry was published in 1957 and his first collection of poetry, *Where We Are* (Charioteer Press), appeared in 1962. Three more collections would follow: *The Anatomy of Love and Other Poems* (Roman Books, 1964); *Mr. Clean and Other Poems* (Amber House Press, 1964); and *Lines to the South and Other Poems* (Louisiana State University Press, 1965), all published while Corrington was teaching in the English Department at LSU, working on his doctorate, and getting his first novel underway. During his early years as a poet, Corrington discovered the poetry of Charles Bukowski, a poet whose work still receives attention today. Corrington wrote several admiring essays about Bukowski's poetry and was active in seeing Bukowski's first major collection of poetry published. For Corrington's extensive correspondence with Bukowski spanning the 1960s, *see* James R. Elkins (ed.), *The John William Corrington & Charles Bukowski Correspondence on Poetry and Writing*, 27 Legal Stud. F. 561 (2003).

Corrington's early promise as a poet was displaced by his intense desire to write major fiction. Corrington's impressive first novel, *And Wait for the Night*, was published in 1964, and after he joined the faculty at Loyola–New Orleans, Corrington published two additional novels, *The Upper Hand* (Putnam, 1967) and *The Bombardier* (Lancer Books, 1970), as the '60s decade came to an end.

In the late '60s, Corrington's fiction came to the attention of film director/producer Roger Corman who approached Corrington about doing a screenplay about the German WW I pilot Manfred von

Richthofen ("The Red Baron"). Corrington, never one to say no to a new writing venture, talked his wife, Joyce, a chemistry professor, into working on the script with him. They wrote *Von Richthofen and Brown* (later released as *The Red Baron*), delivering the finished script to Corman in 1969. The film was released by United Artists in 1971. Corrington's "legal fiction" and stories published before Corrington became a lawyer are found in Joyce Corrington (ed.), *The Collected Stories of John William Corrington* (University of Missouri Press, 1990).

In addition to his '60s novels, the screenwriting venture with Joyce, and his four published collections of poetry, Corrington published his first collection of short stories, *The Lonesome Traveler and Other Stories*, in 1968 and continued to write short fiction throughout his life. During his years as an English professor, Corrington also published academic articles and essays (and wrote, but left unpublished, theoretical and philosophical writings). Some of Corrington's abandoned writings were published in a *Legal Studies Forum* issue titled *Fishing Deep Waters: John William Corrington (1932–1988)* in 2002.

The work with Roger Corman continued in the early 1970s, and the Corringtons—working together as they did on all of Corrington's film scripts—followed up the film script for *Von Richthofen and Brown* (1971) with the following: *The Omega Man* (1970), *Boxcar Bertha* (1971), *The Arena* (1972).

Corrington, who had never developed a great passion for teaching, growing increasingly disaffected with the situation at Loyola–New Orleans where he was battling with the Jesuits over tenure decisions in his English Department, decided to take up the study of law. It was, according to Corrington's own account, his reading of the political philosopher Eric Voegelin that prompted his interest in the study of law.

Bill Corrington was most definitely not the typical first-year law student. When he arrived at Tulane Law School in 1972, he was forty years old, a well-published poet and novelist, a screenwriter, accomplished scholar, chair of an English department. Attending law school seems not to have left Corrington short of time and energy for his writing pursuits. During his first year of law school, Bill Corrington and Joyce wrote the film script for *The Battle for the Planet of the Apes* (1973), and then, in his second year at Tulane, they finished work on another film script, *The Killer Bees* (1974).

Corrington graduated from Tulane Law School in 1975, joined a small New Orleans personal injury law firm, Plotkin & Bradley, and spent the next three years practicing law. He would never return to teaching, although he sometimes considered the possibility, thinking he might make his way back to Shreveport, or settle somewhere in the South.

Corrington gave up the practice of law in 1978 to work with Joyce as head writers for the TV daytime drama *Search for Tomorrow* (CBS). From 1978 to 1988, the Corringtons wrote scripts for *Search for Tomorrow* (CBS) (1978–1980) (477 episodes); *Another World* (1980) (NBC) (23 episodes); *Texas* (1980–1982) (NBC) (147 episodes) (a series they created and wrote); *General Hospital* (1982) (ABC) (54 episodes); *Capitol* (1982–1983) (CBS) (167 episodes); *One Life to Live* (1984) (ABC) (98 episodes);

and finally, *Superior Court* (1986–1989) (238 episodes) (a syndicated series).

During the final decade of his life, the decade he worked as a writer of daytime TV dramas, Corrington published his last major novel, *Shad Sentell* (1984); a collection of short stories, *The Southern Reporter* (1981); and two magnificent novellas featuring lawyers, "Decoration Day" and "The Risi's Wife," collected in *All My Trials* (1987).

Corrington, always open to new ventures for his writing, eventually turned to the detective genre. With a contract from Viking Press, Corrington, in partnership with Joyce, began a series of books that featured a New Orleans police detective—Ralph "Rat" Trapp, a reporter named Wesley Colvin, and a love interest for Colvin, Denise Lemoyne, who begins as a relatively insignificant character but becomes Colvin's lover and eventually an Assistant District Attorney. The first of the Corringtons' police detective, mystery novels, *So Small a Carnival*, appeared in 1986, with *A Project Named Desire* and *A Civil Death* to follow in 1987. The fourth and final book in the series, *The White Zone*, was published in 1990, after Bill Corrington's death in 1988. (All of the detective fiction was published by Viking.)

6   After taking up the study of law, Corrington began to find a place for lawyers and judges in his fiction. "The Actes and Monuments," Corrington's first lawyer story, was published in *Sewanee Review* in 1975, the year he finished law school. A second lawyer story, "Pleadings," was published in 1976 in the *Southern Review*, appearing during Corrington's first year as a practicing lawyer. A third story, "Every Act Whatever

of Man," appeared in the *Southern Review* in 1978, this one in the final year of his law practice. Corrington continued, throughout the 1980s, until his death in 1988, to make the lives of lawyers and judges a part of his fiction.

7   I was not the first to see the value of Corrington's writings. William Domnarski, who taught Law and Literature at the University of Connecticut, preceded me in the discovery of Corrington's work. *See* William Domnarski, *A Novelist's Knowing Look at the Law*, 69 A.B.A. J. 1706 (1983) [reprinted in 32 Legal Stud. F. 839 (2002)]; William Domnarski, "Corrington's Lawyer as Moralist," *in* William Mills (ed.), *John William Corrington: Southern Man of Letters* 144–155 (University of Central Arkansas Press, 1994) [reprinted in 32 Legal Stud. F. 847 (2002)]; William Domnarski, *Law and Literature*, 27 Legal Stud. F. 109 (2003).

The only other reference in the legal literature to Corrington's work that preceded my discovery of Corrington I have been able to locate is a book review of a Corrington collection of stories, *The Actes and Monuments* (University of Illinois Press, 1978). *See* Judith L. Maute, *Book Review*, 37 Okla. L. Rev. 635 (1984). Maute was an Assistant Professor at the University of Oklahoma when the Corrington book review was published. Corrington made one of his few public presentations to a law school audience at the University of Oklahoma on January 31, 1985, where he appeared, with Judith Koffler, at a University of Oklahoma College of Law Enrichment Program. Corrington's Oklahoma invitation seems to have been initiated by Professor Drew Kersen. A copy of Corrington's Oklahoma presentation, titled "Logos, Lex, and Law" was located in his papers (housed at Centenary College in Shreveport, Louisiana) and first published in the *Legal Studies Forum*. See John William Corrington, *Logos, Lex, and Law*, 26 Legal Stud. F. 709 (2002). A video of the Corrington presentation at the University of Oklahoma exists but the quality of the VHS recording is extremely poor.

8 It was reading the work of John William Corrington that prompted me to sail where the strong wind took me. In 2002, the *Legal Studies Forum*, with the gracious permission and essential assistance of Joyce Corrington, republished Bill Corrington's lawyer stories, a selection of his published and unpublished essays, and republished commentaries about his work and his life: A special issue was devoted to Corrington's fiction—*Fiction by John William Corrington*, 26 Legal Stud. F. 1–492 (2002). A second issue focused on Corrington's non-fiction work—*Fishing Deep Waters: John William Corrington (1932–1988)*, 26 Legal Stud. F. 493–912 (2002). A substantial part of a third *LSF* issue featured Corrington's poetry, 27 Legal Stud. F. 493–680 (2003) (the 2003 *LSF* issue included a personal note on Corrington's poetry by Jo LeCoeur; an essay on the writing of Corrington's last novel, *Shad Sentell* by Lloyd Halliburton, a childhood friend of Corrington; a bibliography of Corrington's published poetry compiled by Joyce Corrington). My efforts to publish John William Corrington's work would not have been possible without Joyce Corrington's permission, and would have suffered in more ways

than one, without her constant encouragement. Joyce Corrington's assistance and advice on matters involving her husband was invaluable.

9   An interviewer of John William Corrington in 1975 observes that "Corrington has squeezed into one lifetime what most of us might not manage in two or three." Louis Gallo, "Corrington: From Poetry to 'Killer Bees,'" *The Courier: New Orleans Journal of Leisure, Entertainment and the Arts* II (Nov. 27–Dec. 3, 1975).

10 When I left the Department of Justice in Washington, D.C., my friends Winston Miller and Marvin Coan, knowing my affection for Justice Douglas, presented me with a copy of William O. Douglas's *Go East Young Man—The Early Years: The Autobiography of William O. Douglas* (Random House, 1944) signed by Justice Douglas.

11 Charles L. Black's poetry: *Poems by Charles Black*, 111 Yale L. J. 1927 (2002) (selected by David Black) (The *Yale Law Journal* memorial was also published, by the *Columbia Law Review*, 102 Colum. L. Rev. 896 (2002)). Black's published poetry includes: *The Waking: Passenger* (New Orleans Poetry Journal Press Book, 1983); *Owls Bay in Brooklyn* (Dustbooks, 1980); *Telescopes and Islands: Poems* (Hassell Street Press, 2021) (AMS Press, 1975) (Alan Swallow, 1963).

12 The originality in John Batt's writing can be seen in Batt's essays: *The New Outlaw: A Psychological Footnote to the Criminal Law*, 52 Ky. L.J. 497 (1963–1964); *Notes from the Penal Colony: A Jurisprudence beyond Good and Evil*, 50 Iowa L. Rev.

999 (1965) (published just two years prior to my first exposure to John Batt's teaching); *They Shoot Horses, Don't They: An Essay on the Scotoma of One-Eyed Kings*, 15 UCLA L. Rev. 510 (1968) (published the year, 1967–1968, when I was a student in Batt's Criminal Law course); *Law, Science, and Narrative: Reflections on Brain Science, Electronic Media, Story, and Law Learning*, 40 J. Legal Educ. 19 (1990) (an article I solicited from my friend John Batt for a symposium issue of the *Journal of Legal Education* I edited: "Pedagogy of Narrative: A Symposium—Reflections on Storytelling and Narrative"); *American Legal Populism: A Jurisprudential and Historical Narrative, Including Reflections on Critical Legal Studies*, 22 N. Ky. L. Rev. 651 (1995). I took every course that John Batt taught during my days as a law student. I readily acknowledge John Batt's influence on my teaching and writing.

II

identifying our lawyer poets

WITH THE QUEST to see what I can learn about Corrington's fiction, his scholarly writing, and his time as a lawyer in New Orleans underway, I continue to puzzle over what it might mean to be a lawyer and a poet. I didn't find my puzzlement addressed in reading Corrington's poetry.[1] Corrington himself seems to have never focused on how being a poet and a lawyer might reflect entirely different sensibilities. So, here is what I know: John William Corrington was a poet. And, I happen to know of two other lawyer poets: Wallace Stevens[2] and Archibald MacLeish.[3] I'm tempted to say everyone knows about Wallace Stevens. Even law colleagues take quizzical note of Wallace Stevens's enterprising, mind-bending, dual careers—modernist poet and insurance company lawyer. Oddly enough, in the literary world, Stevens is more frequently identified as an insurance executive than he is a lawyer. Stevens, it appears, regarded himself as a lawyer rather than an insurance company executive.

Archibald MacLeish first came to my attention in reading I was doing for the Lawyers and Literature seminar I taught for many years.[4] MacLeish, a Harvard Law

School graduate, practiced law for three years (as did Corrington) and was on his way to a promising career as a Boston lawyer, and by some accounts, an assured position on the Harvard Law School faculty, when he abandoned the legal profession and moved to Paris in pursuit of his life as a poet. (MacLeish would later become a playwright, journalist, statesman, and Librarian of Congress.) But MacLeish would not forget, in a long and distinguished career, that he had studied to be a lawyer. In his eighties, MacLeish published an "Apologia" in the *Harvard Law Review* in which he praised his law school education.[5] MacLeish relates in "Apologia" his impression that his law colleagues found him more than a little odd for having abandoned the legal profession, all the more odd that the reason he left the practice of law was to pursue poetry. I suspect there is some lingering sense of this oddness MacLeish describes that accounts for my interest in lawyer poets over the past twenty-four years.

After a summer reading Corrington, I decide to write about this poet who becomes a lawyer. For that writing, I could have delved into the prolific writings by and about Wallace Stevens and Archibald MacLeish, studied what they had to say about their dual endeavors in the world of law and poetry, and moved on to other writing projects. But this is not the course I pursued. Of course, I didn't know what course I was pursuing and that makes it hard to know where my fascination with Corrington, and by way of Corrington with lawyer poets, might end up taking me.

I mention my interest in Corrington and my puzzlement about lawyer poets to my friend Lowell Komie, a Chicago lawyer and author.[6] Lowell and I corresponded for years after he discovered I was teaching a good number of his short stories in my Lawyers and Literature seminar. Komie pointed out that Edgar Lee Masters, famed for his *Spoon River Anthology*, was a lawyer.[7] I would later learn that Masters practiced law for almost a decade with the infamous Clarence Darrow, and that, at one time, Ernest McGaffey, still another lawyer poet, was in the firm with Masters and Darrow.[8]

Komie alerted me to still another well-known poet associated with law—Charles Reznikoff—who figures prominently in the history of Modernist poets.[9] Reznikoff, born in Brooklyn in 1894, attended the University of Missouri School of Journalism for a year, long enough to learn he didn't want to be a journalist. He studied law at New York University and was admitted to the New York bar in 1916. Reznikoff took additional law courses at Columbia University, but his efforts at law practice faltered, and he took a variety of menial jobs to support himself. In 1928, he joined the editorial staff at the American Law Book Company, at that time, publisher of a multi-volume legal encyclopedia, *Corpus Juris*: an encyclopedia well known to law students of my era that is a discarded historical relic of a pre-digital era. A law student quizzed today would have no idea that *Corpus Juris*, and its later edition, *Corpus Juris Secundum*, were at one time standard legal reference works. Reznikoff worked as a legal editor to sustain himself as a writer and a poet; learning to use a printing press, Reznikoff set the type and printed much of his early poetry. Reznikoff became the only significant poet of the twentieth century to make extensive use of judicial opinions in his poetry.

My correspondence with Lowell Komie, learning about Edgar Lee Masters and Charles Reznikoff, left me curious. There must be other lawyer poets. Has anyone tried to identify who they are? A friend on the staff at the Tarlton Law Library at the University of Texas–Austin,

Marlyn Robinson,[10] informed of my newly minted interest, spurred my interest further when she presented me with a small list of lawyer poets she had uncovered (with a single exception, all historical figures). The name of the single contemporary poet on Robinson's list, Michael Blumenthal, would later become a valued friend and colleague.[11] Marlyn made no claim that her list was anything more than a cursory survey to present some obvious names for me.

The identification of the first twenty lawyer poets produced some interesting literary figures: Joel Barlow (1754–1812). Royall Tyler (1757–1826). William Cullen Bryant (1794–1878). Charles Fenno Hoffman (1806–1844). William Gilmore Simms (1806–1870). James Russell Lowell (1819–1891). Sidney Lanier (1842–1881). Famous jurists and two presidents: Joseph Story (1779–1845) and Salmon P. Chase (1808–1873). John Quincy Adams (1767–1848) and Abraham Lincoln (1809–1865). Story and Chase are historical figures in legal scholarly circles who have a recognized place in legal history. Abraham Lincoln's affinity for poetry is widely known, John Quincy Adams perhaps less so.[12] The literary figures, well known in literary circles with established associations with the legal profession, were unknown to me. The Marlyn Robinson list and the names I began to uncover enticed me to pursue the search and produce what would eventually become an exhaustive catalogue of lawyer poets.[13]

Following up on the Marlyn Robinson first list of lawyer poets, I saw a reference on abebooks.com to a poetry anthology edited by a nineteenth-century poet lawyer, William Cullen Bryant, one of the lawyer poets on the Robinson list.[14] The William Cullen Bryant anthology was being offered for sale by a local used bookstore in

Morgantown, West Virginia. A ten-minute walk and I had acquired William Cullen Bryant's *The Family Library of Poetry and Song Being Choice Selections from the Best Poets, English, Scottish, Irish, and American; Including Translations from Ancient and Modern Languages*—a fitting long title for a 920-page poetry anthology. My copy of Bryant's *Library of Poetry and Song*, published in 1886 (first published in 1870), cost me $25.60. The anthology, adorned with an engraved cover and iconic image of William Cullen Bryant, is a massive book. My Bryant anthology, having survived for over one hundred thirty years, has boards with warning signs of detachment, but the binding holds sturdy for a volume this size, this old. With the William Cullen Bryant anthology, a book of some *antiquarian* appeal, I began to acquire other old poetry anthologies and eventually the old books of the lawyer poets themselves. I learned that old-book dealers continue to warehouse these long-abandoned books.

My major complaint with the William Cullen Bryant anthology was the absence of bios of the poets. I fared better with my next acquisition—Rufus Wilmot Griswold's equally massive *Poets of America* (1872). The Griswold anthology contained bios, which allowed me to significantly expand the short-list of lawyer poets that Marlyn Robinson compiled. Perusing a tattered, decaying copy of the Griswold anthology I identified a substantial number of lawyer poets to add to the catalogue I was compiling: St. George Tucker (1750–1837), John Trumbull (1750–1831), Joel Barlow (1755–1812), St. John Honeywood (1765–1798), John Quincy Adams (1767–1848), Joseph Hopkinson (1770–1842), Robert Treat Pain Jr. (1773–1811), William Munford (1775–1825), Francis S. Key (1779–1843),

John Pierpont (1785–1866), Richard Henry Wilde (1789–1847), Alexander H. Everett (1790–1847), Seba Smith (1792–1868), John Neal (1793–1876), John G. C. Brainard (1796–1828), Robert C. Sands (1799–1832), William B. O. Peabody (1799–1848), Grenville Mellen (1799–1841), George W. Cutter (1801–1865), Edward C. Pinkney (1802–1828), Fortunatus Cosby Jr. (1802–1871), Albert G. Greene (1802–1868), Rufus Dawes (1803–1859), Otway Curry (1804–1855), Charles Fenno Hoffman (1806–1844), William Gilmore Simms (1806–1870), Micah P. Flint (1807–1830), N. P. Willis (1807–1830), George Lunt (1807–1885), Theodore S. Fay (1807–1898), Edward Sanford (1807–1876), B. B. Thatcher (1809–1840), Albert Pike (1809–1891, Park Benjamin (1809–1864), Isaac McLellan Jr. (1810–1899), Robert T. Conrad (1810–1858), Henry R. Jackson (1810–1898), Alfred B. Street (1811–1881), W. H. C. Hosmer (1814–1877), Cornelius Mathews (1815–1889), Richard H. Dana Jr. (1815–1882), Philip Pendleton Cooke (1816–1850), John G. Saxe (1816–1887), Henry B. Hirst (1817–1874), E. Spencer Miller (1817–1878), William Wallace (1819–1881), James Russell Lowell (1819–1891), Thomas Dunn English (1819–1902), John R. Thompson (1823–1873), William Allen Butler (1825–1902), and John Esten Cooke (1830–1886). (Additional lawyer poets whose work appears in Griswold's *Poets of America* anthology without a bio include: William Wetmore Story (1819–1895), Henry Howard Brownell (1820–1872), Henry Timrod (1828–1867), Paul Hamilton Hayne (1830–1886), John Aylmer Dorgan (1836–1867), William Winter (1836–1917), Robert Kelley Weeks (1840–1876).

During the early months working on the lawyer poets excavation project, I continue to acquire nineteenth-century poetry anthologies that provide additional names and bios for the catalogue of lawyer poets. No one, so far as I could determine, had ever attempted an extensive identification of America's lawyer poets. No one, I suspect, had ever had reason to engage in such a project. I'm not at all sure that this account of how I ended up pursuing this lawyer poets identification project establishes a reason for doing it.

Expanding the effort to identify our lawyer poets, I began to discover names that could only loosely be called historical figures, names of lawyer poets that history would leave us with little to remember. The poetry of most of these lawyers is of little interest to anyone today.[15] What took me by surprise was not the poetry I was finding but the delight I experienced in identifying these obscure lawyer poets, a delight enhanced by acquiring their published work. (I found far more of this forgotten work of lawyer poets to be available than I would ever have imagined.[16])

Compiling this first historical catalogue of lawyer poets, the vast number of them obscure, I had a sense I was excavating these literary lawyers—lives lived in two dramatically diverse worlds—from the debris of history.[17] I began to fantasize a new history of "lawyers and literature," a history in which obscure lawyer poets would stand, alongside better-known historical figures like Wallace Stevens, Charles Reznikoff, and Edgar Lee Masters, to give us a new perspective on what is now known as the "law and literature" movement.[18] Lawyer poets, obscure as they may be, would have their own claim to history.

Focusing on lives of lawyer poets—Wallace Stevens, Archibald MacLeish, Edgar Lee Masters, Charles Reznikoff—and yes, John William Corrington and hundreds of others—we might pursue "law and literature" not only as a study of representations of law and lawyers in literature, but a study of how a life steeped in literature *and* in law can be lived.[19] I was curious: How do the demands and pleasures of one world—law—carry over into the poetry world? What does the poet bring to the practice of law? How do lawyer poets make sense of a life in which these two diverse endeavors are undertaken? How is this life of duality to be imagined—lived?

Over several months, I put together a substantial catalogue of lawyers who pursued their interest in poetry, poets who found their way into the legal profession. I created a website with a web page (with bios and bibliographies of published work) for every lawyer poet I had been able to identify. The website, Strangers to Us All: Lawyers and Poetry, was posted on September 3, 2001, and is currently available online through the web directory at lawlit.net.

From our earliest days as a nation—still earlier in England, Ireland, Scotland, Wales, and the vast world beyond Europe—we find lawyers who are poets—poets who engage in the practice of law. Lawyer poets have served as president, and sat as justices on the Supreme Court and on state supreme courts. They have served in the Cabinet and as governors and attorney generals of the various states. They have been elected to Congress. Some of the early women lawyers and African American lawyers in the United States, surmounting obstacles we recall today with shame, were poets. Our lawyer poets have been journalists, politicians, ministers, physicians, novelists, sculptors, scholars, presidents of universities, generals (and foot soldiers) in the Confederate and

Union armies, law professors, duelists, famous Masons, and poet laureates.

Lawyer poets, far more prevalent in our history than previously acknowledged, are presented to us in plain view in aging poetry anthologies. Consider Armistead C. Gordon Jr.'s *Virginia Writers of Fugitive Verse* (J. T. White & Co., 1923) (published almost fifty years after the appearance of the William Cullen Bryant and Rufus Wilmot Griswold anthologies). Gordon prefaces his anthology with the claim that the South has been a congenial place for poets, and that as of 1922, when his anthology was published, there were still nineteenth-century Southern poets well remembered in the South.[20] Gordon notes, in the opening sentences of his preface:

> What knowledge the reading public at large may have of Southern poetry is doubtless due not so much to the work of any one author, Poe and Lanier excepted, as to the numerous and fugitive poems which Southern writers have produced. Key's "Star-Spangled Banner," Wilde's "My Life is Like the Summer Rose," O'Hara's "Bivouac of the Dead," St. George Tucker's "Resignation," Randall's "Maryland, My Maryland," Pinkney's "A Health," Ticknor's "Little Giffen of Tennessee," and P. P. Cooke's "Florence Vane" form a galaxy of which any literature might be proud, and which a collection of the great mono-poems of literature would be most likely to include.[21]

Most striking, in Gordon's early 1920s compilation of singularly notable Southern poems, is the fact that of the two great poets mentioned, Edgar Allen Poe and Sidney Lanier, one of them, Lanier, began his career as a lawyer. Of the authors of memorable poems selected for the Gordon anthology—Francis Scott Key (1779–1843), Richard Henry Wilde (1789–1847), Theodore O'Hara (1820–1867), St. George Tucker (1752–1828), Edward Coate Pinkney (1802–1828), Philip Pendleton Cooke (1816–1850), James Ryder Randall (1839–1908), and Francis Orray Ticknor (1822–1874)—every poet Gordon mentions in the preface to his anthology, except James Ryder Randall, who taught English literature and was a newspaper editor, and Francis Orray Ticknor, who was a country doctor in Georgia, had been trained as a lawyer or practiced law. Gordon himself, oddly, makes no reference to the fact that so many of the poets on his list were lawyers. Perhaps to Gordon, in 1922, being a lawyer and a poet were not so remarkable to need acknowledgment. Curious perhaps, Gordon, the editor of *Virginia Writers of Fugitive Verse* was a lawyer.[22]

Perusing Mildred Lewis Rutherford's *The South in History and Literature* (Franklin-Turner, 1906), we find another claim for the importance of Southern literature, especially literature produced before the Civil War. In Rutherford's introduction there is again reference to Edgar Allen Poe, who was not a lawyer, and to significant literary lawyer poets—Francis Scott Key (1779–1843) (the celebrated author of the "Star-Spangled Banner"), Theodore O'Hara (1820–1867) ("The Bivouac of the Dead," a poem written in memory of those who fell at the Battle of Buena Vista), and Richard Henry Wilde (1789–1847)—all lawyers included in Armistead Gordon's *Virginia Writers of Fugitive Verse*. Rutherford goes on to name still other memorable Southern lawyer poets whose poetry appears before 1860, most notably Albert Pike (1809–1891) and John Pendleton Kennedy (1795–1870). In looking at the period after the Civil War,

Rutherford points to Sidney Lanier (1842–1881), the most notable lawyer poet of the Civil War era ("unquestionably one of the greatest poets this country ever produced") and Henry Timrod (1828–1867), another Civil War poet. Lanier and Timrod were both, at one time, lawyers, although they are today remembered for their literary pursuits.

■

Many of the lawyer poets I identified were unearthed in the crumbling pages of nineteenth-century poetry anthologies. Surrounding myself with *antiquarian* poetry anthologies seemed to lend credence to the idea I was doing historical work.[23] It may be true that the long-forgotten lawyer poets speak to us with their poetry, but it was not their poetry but their existence—their lives—that intrigued me. Whatever they may have left us in their poetry and other writings must suffer the ever-present silence of history. The old lawyers, in their poetry, are ghosts who speak their own language.

Chapter II
Endnotes

1. John William Corrington's poetry was first published in 1957 and his first collection of poetry, *Where We Are* (Charioteer Press) appeared in 1962. Three more collections would follow: *The Anatomy of Love and Other Poems* (Amber House Press, 1964), *Mr. Clean and Other Poems* (Roman Books, 1964), and *Lines to the South and Other Poems* (Louisiana State University Press, 1965), all published while Corrington was teaching in the English Department at LSU, working on his doctorate, and his first novel. *Lines to the South and Other Poems* would be Corrington's final published collection of poetry. For my selection from Corrington's published poetry, *see* John William Corrington, *Poetry*, 27 Legal Stud. F. 511–560 (2003).

2. Wallace Stevens (1879–1955): For those interested in how Wallace Stevens's work as a poet and a lawyer is viewed in scholarly legal circles, *see* Thomas Grey, *The Wallace Stevens Case: Law and the Practice of Poetry* (Harvard University Press, 1991); Thomas C. Grey, *Hear the Other Side: Wallace Stevens and Pragmatist Legal Theory*, 63 S. Cal. L. Rev. 1569 (1990); Thomas C. Grey, *Steel against Intimation: The Motive for Metaphor of Wallace Stevens, Esq.*, 2 Yale J.L. & Human. 231 (1990); Daniel J. Kornstein, *The Double Life of Wallace Stevens: Is Law Ever the "Necessary Angel" of Creative Art?* 41 N.Y.L. Sch. L. Rev. 1187 (1997); David Lavery, *Imagination and Insurance: Wallace Stevens and Benjamin Lee Whorf at the Hartford*, 24 Legal Stud.

F. 481 (2000); Joe Johnston, *We Do Not Talk Poetry Here: Wallace Stevens and the Practice of Poetry, Law, and Life*, 19 (2) Experience 36 (2009); Steven T. Knight, *Philanthropists among the Lawyers: The Law School Journal of Wallace Stevens*, 4 ALSA F. 51 (1979–1980); and Nelson F. Crouch, *Mysterious Crossings*, 27 Legal Stud. F. 681 (2003).

For engaging readable sources on Wallace Stevens, see Peter Brazeau's oral biography, *Parts of a World: Wallace Stevens Remembered* (Random House, 1983) and the Holly Stevens collection of her father's letters, *Letters of Wallace Stevens* (University of California Press, 1996).

3   Archibald MacLeish (1892–1982): For an introduction to MacLeish and his life, see R. H. Winnick (ed.), *Letters of Archibald MacLeish 1907 to 1982* (Houghton Mifflin, 1983); Scott Donaldson, *Archibald MacLeish: An American Life* (Houghton Mifflin Co., 1992).

4   For a book-length account of the Lawyers and Literature seminar, see James R. Elkins, *Lawyers and Literature: Reflections on a Course of Reading*, 44 Legal Stud. F. 1–176 (2020).

5   Archibald MacLeish, *Apologia*, 85 Harv. L. Rev. 1505 (1972) (reprinted in Archibald MacLeish, *Riders on the Earth: Essays and Recollections* 82–88 (Houghton Mifflin, 1978)). Law colleagues, especially those well versed in "law and literature" scholarship may have chanced upon Archibald MacLeish's short, intriguing "Apologia"—published over fifty years ago—in which we were alerted to MacLeish's Harvard Law School education and his brief years as a Boston lawyer.

6   On my friend Lowell Komie, another distinguished undiscovered writer of legal fiction, *see* James R. Elkins, *Lowell B. Komie of Chicago—Writer and Lawyer*, 25 Legal Stud. F. 1 (2001) and *Lowell B. Komie: An Interview*, 25 Legal Stud. F. 223 (2001). For Komie's legal fiction, *see* Lowell B. Komie, *The Legal Fiction of Lowell B. Komie* (Swordfish/Chicago, 2005). Komie's legal fiction was earlier collected and published in an issue of the *Legal Studies Forum*—The Legal Fiction of Lowell B. Komie, 25 Legal Stud. F. 11–213 (2001). Komie was initially reluctant to have his legal fiction published apart from his other stories. With some considerable effort, I finally persuaded Lowell that legal fiction did not have the questionable reputation that he feared it might have. After publication of the *LSF* issue devoted to his legal fiction in 2001, Lowell published the collection under his own imprint in 2005. At Lowell's insistence, I wrote an introduction to the collection.

7   Edgar Lee Masters (1868–1950): Edgar Lee Masters, *Spoon River Anthology* (Macmillan Co., 1915) (University of Illinois Press, annotated ed., 1992) (John E. Hallwas ed.). Edgar Lee Masters wrote an interesting autobiography, *Across Spoon River: An Autobiography* (Farrar & Rinehart, 1936) (Octagon Books, 1969) (University of Illinois Press, 1991), but the sweep and pathos of Masters's life is best portrayed in a masterful biography of Masters—Herbert K. Russell, *Edgar Lee Masters: A Biography* (University of Illinois Press, 2001)—that appeared as my interest in lawyer poets was getting underway.

Masters practiced law with Clarence Darrow from 1903 to 1911. Darrow had, we learn from a reading of Masters's involvement with him, rather peculiar notions of ethics and friendship. On Darrow's ethics, *see* Gerald F. Uelmen, *Fighting Fire with Fire: A Reflection on the Ethics of Clarence Darrow*, 71 Fordham L. Rev. 1543 (2003). Masters, like the more well-known Wallace Stevens, has received attention in legal scholarly circles: John V. Orth, *The Law in Spoon River*, 16 (3) Legal Stud. F. 301 (1992); Steven Richman, *Edgar Lee Masters and the Poetics of Legal Realism*, 31 Cal. W. L. Rev. 103 (1994); Michael Stanford, *The Cyclopean Eye, The Courtly Game, Admissions Against Interest: Five Modern American Lawyer Poets*, 30 Legal Stud. F. 9, 11–20 (2006) (focusing on Edgar Lee Masters, Brad Leithauser, Lawrence Joseph, and Martín Espada, with commentary on both Archibald MacLeish and Wallace Stevens); Randall Tietjen, *Clarence Darrow & Edgar Lee Masters*, 13 Green Bag 2d 411 (2010).

8   Ernest McGaffey (1861–1941): Edgar Lee Masters practiced with a number of different lawyers, including Ernest McGaffey, before he joined Darrow in the practice of law in 1903. (The Masters-Darrow partnership continued until 1911.)

Masters, at one time, shared an apartment with McGaffey, who encouraged his writing. McGaffey was, reputedly "a restless spirit" and remained with Masters and his then partner, Kickham Scanland, in the practice of law for only a year. Herbert K. Russell, *Edgar Lee Masters: A Biography* 37–38 (University of Illinois Press, 2001). Masters's first volume of poetry, *A Book of Verses* (1898), came about, in part, because McGaffey, his roommate, law associate, and fellow poet, urged its publication. *Id.* at 58. McGaffey seems to have played a part in Masters's "look homeward for literary material"; Masters and McGaffey spent several days in 1894 in Spoon River country exploring the towns and countryside that Masters would memorialize in his autobiography. *Id.* at 66. McGaffey returned to live in the area some ten years later.

Oscar Fay Adams, in his *Dictionary of American Authors*, identifies McGaffey as "[a] lawyer of Chicago" in an all-too-brief bio. Oscar Fay Adams, *A Dictionary of American Authors* 242 (Houghton, Mifflin & Co., 1899). McGaffey is a lawyer poet of whom I have been able to learn quite little. Edmund Clarence Stedman (ed.), *An American Anthology 1787–1899* 809 (Houghton, Mifflin & Co., 1900) provides this brief bio: "MCGAFFEY, Ernest, lawyer, b. London, O[hio]., 1861. Now a resident of Chicago, Ill., where he practises his profession. Besides being identified as an author, Mr. McGaffey has standing as a sportsman and celebrant of the gun and rod."

McGaffey's poetry, published over a period of some thirty years, includes: Ernest McGaffey, *Poems of Gun and Rod* (C. Scribner's Sons, 1892); *Poems* (Dodd, Mead & Co., 1895); *A California Idyl* (Channing Auxiliary, 1899) (illustrations by William H. Bull); *Cosmos* (The Philosopher Press, 1903); *Sonnets to a Wife* (W. M. Reedy, 1901) (W. M. Reedy, 1905) (Printed by Wolfer & Co., 1922); *Poems of the Town* (R. G. Badger & Co., 1901); *Ballades and Idyls* (Saturday Night Pub. Co., 1931); *Ballades* (Graphic Press, 1938); and *War* (Lymanhouse, 1939).

Working on the manuscript for *Discovering Our Lawyer Poets*, I learn that my reclusive neighbor and friend Bradley Omanson is an Edgar Lee Masters aficionado. I lived next door to Bradley for several decades before I learned he was a poet, a poet whose work I enjoy reading. For Omanson's "Masters's influence" poems, *see* BJ Omanson, *Stark County Poems* (Monongahela Books, enlarged ed., 2020).

9 Charles Reznikoff (1884–1976): For an autobiographical account of Reznikoff's life, *see* Charles Reznikoff, *By the Well of Living & Seeing: New & Selected Poems 1918–1973* 129–140 (Black Sparrow Press, 1974); Milton Hindus (ed.), *Charles Reznikoff: Man and Poet* (National Poetry Foundation, University of Maine at Orono, 1984). To date there is no biography of Reznikoff; the standard reference is Milton Hindus (ed.), *Charles Reznikoff: Man and Poet* (National Poetry Foundation, 1984) and Milton Hindus (ed.), *Selected Letters of Charles Reznikoff 1917–1976* (Black Sparrow Press, 1997). For Reznikoff's prose poem account of his days as a law student, *see* Charles Reznikoff, *By the Well of Living & Seeing*, at 129–132.

Charles Reznikoff's law-influenced poetry includes: *Testimony: The United States (1885–1890)–Recitative* (New Directions/San Francisco Review, 1965) and *Testimony: The United States (1891–1900)* (Charles Reznikoff, 1968). For commentary on Reznikoff's law-related poetry, *see* Benjamin Watson, *Reznikoff's Testimony*, 82 Law Lib. J. 647 (1990) [reprinted: 29 Legal Stud. F. 67 (2005)] and Michael Stanford, *The Cyclopean Eye, the Courtly Game, Admissions Against Interest: Five*

Modern American Lawyer Poets, 30 Legal Stud. F. 9, 20–30 (2006).

10 A tribute to my colleague Marlyn Robinson (1947–2014): Marlyn Robinson was one of the few academic colleagues to express an interest in my fascination with lawyer poets, and, although I never met her, I enjoyed our correspondence and our friendship. Marlyn Robinson—you were a fine colleague and an inspiration.

11 The list of lawyer poets that Marlyn Robinson presented to me was confined, with a single exception, to historical figures. Robinson related to me that she had read about a poet, Michael Blumenthal, who had at one time been a lawyer and was currently teaching in Austin. Marlyn thought Blumenthal might be someone I would want to talk with about lawyer poets. With many twists and turns in the road, I end up, in 2007, publishing a *Legal Studies Forum* issue devoted to Michael Blumenthal's work (including his poetry): *Correcting the World: Selected Poetry and Writing of Michael Blumenthal*, 31 Legal Stud. F. 1–447 (2007). Blumenthal explains his decision to abandon the legal profession and take up his life as a writer, poet, and teacher in his essay, "The Road Not Taken—Twice," in 31 Legal Stud. F. 1 (2007). My work with Michael led to his move to Morgantown, West Virginia, where he served with me for six years on the college of law faculty. Michael has recently moved from Morgantown to Washington, D.C.; he continues to spend summers in Hungary.

Michael Blumenthal (1949–   ) was born in Vineland, New Jersey. He attended State University of New York at Binghamton where he studied philosophy. After graduating from college, he taught

German at a school for emotionally disturbed adolescents. He received his law degree from Cornell in 1974 and joined the Federal Trade Commission as a lawyer (1974–1975). He left the FTC to become an arts administrator with the National Endowment for the Arts (1975–1976) and then editor at TimeLife Books (1977–1980). He returned to the National Endowment for the Humanities in 1980 as assistant to the chairman, a position he held until 1981. Blumenthal was a lecturer in poetry at Harvard University and director of creative writing at Harvard. From 1992–1996, he was a Senior Fulbright Lecturer in American Literature in Budapest, Hungary, as well as an editor at the Central European University Press. From 1996 to 1997, he taught at the University of Haifa in Israel. In 2004–2005, he held the Acuff Chair of Excellence in the Creative Arts at Austin Peay State University in Tennessee. He spends his summers in a small village near the shores of Lake Balaton in Hungary.

Blumenthal's published poetry includes: *Correcting the World: Poems Selected & New 1980–2024* (Ravenna Press, 2024); *Don't Die: Poems 2013–2021* (Rabbit House Press, 2021); *No Hurry: Poems 2000–2012* (Etruscan Press, 2012); *And* (BOA Editions, 2009); *Dusty Angel: Poems* (BOA Editions, 1999); *The Wages of Goodness: Poems* (University of Missouri Press, 1992); *Against Romance: Poems* (Viking, 1987) (Penguin, 1988) (Pleasure Boat Studio, 2005); *Days We Would Rather Know: Poems* (Viking, 1984) (Penguin, 1984) (Pleasure Boat Studios, 2005); *Laps: A Poem* (University of Massachusetts Press, 1984); and *Sympathetic Magic* (Water Mark Press, 1980). Blumenthal's work is anthologized in Helen Vendler (ed.), *The Harvard Book of Contemporary American Poetry* (Harvard University Press, 1985).

Blumenthal is the author of a memoir: *All My Mothers and Fathers: A Memoir* (HarperCollins, 2002).

12 John Quincy Adams and his "passion for poetry" is front and center of Robert A. Ferguson's *Law and Letters in American Culture* 3–10 (Harvard University Press, 1984). The Ferguson book is required reading for anyone interested in the early days of the republic when lawyers were men of letters and their pursuit of poetry would not have made them odd creatures. My one concern about Ferguson's *Law and Letters in American Culture* is the implication that after the nineteenth century and the onset of changes in the legal profession, the era of the literary lawyer became a historical artifact. Whatever the implications of Ferguson's view of the passing role of literary lawyers, our lawyer poets—citizens of the two worlds—continue to exist, continue to flourish.

13 *See* Appendix: A Chronological Index of Lawyer Poets (c. 1600–1950).

14 William Cullen Bryant (1794–1878): "Poet and editor William Cullen Bryant stood among the most celebrated figures in the frieze of 19th century America. The fame he won as a poet while in his youth remained with him as he entered his 80s; only Henry Wadsworth Longfellow and Ralph Waldo Emerson were his rivals in popularity over the course of his life." William Cullen Bryant [entry], Poetry Foundation (www.poetryfoundation.org).

There is an extensive body of writing on William Cullen Bryant and his literary pursuits. Bryant, we are told, spent a decade in the practice of law: "Having passed ten years in successful practice in the courts, he determined to abandon the uncongenial business of a lawyer, and devote his attention more exclusively to literature." Rufus Wilmot Griswold, *The Poets and Poetry of America* 169–170 (James Miller, Publisher, 1872). *See generally*, Robert A. Ferguson, *Law and Letters in American Culture* 173–195 (Harvard University Press, 1984) (chapter titled: "William Cullen Bryant: The Creative Context of the Poet"); Steven M. Richman, *William Cullen Bryant and the Poetry of Natural Law*, 30 Akron L. Rev. 661 (1997).

15 The scholarly interest in nineteenth-century poetry of lawyers lingers on. *See* Michael H. Hoeflich (ed.), *Anthology of Nineteeth Century American Legal Poetry* (Talbot Publ., 2018); Michael H. Hoeflich, *Charles Davis: Philadelphia Lawyer & Newspaper Poet*, 39 Legal Stud. F. 49 (2015); M. H. Hoeflich & Lawrence Jenab, *Three Lawyer-Poets of the Nineteenth Century*, 8 Green Bag 2d 249 (2005).

16 Reading Stevens, MacLeish, Masters, and Reznikoff, and editing *Legal Studies Forum* issues devoted to John William Corrington, it dawned on me that I had, in finding the lawyer poets, stumbled into an underutilized area of "law and literature" scholarship. In contemporary "law and literature" scholarly writing, the focus is on the representation of law and lawyers in literary work, a focus that largely ignores the lives of men and women who, by fate and disposition, have pursued both law and poetry. Knowing

I would not fully pursue this shift, from "law and literature" to "lawyers and literature," I began to create a library that would provide tangible evidence of a new history of "law and literature" that would include the work of obscure lawyer poets.

17 Literary scholars focusing on the history of poetry in the United States and legal scholars exploring the literary aspirations of this country's lawyers have relied primarily on Robert A. Ferguson's *Law and Letters in American Culture* (Harvard University Press, 1984). For another legal scholar who has pursued historical studies of lawyer poets, see Steven Richman, *Edgar Lee Masters and the Poetics of Legal Realism*, 31 Cal. W. L. Rev. 103 (1994) ("The other principal American lawyerpoets that I have identified are Sidney Lanier, William Cullen Bryant, James Russell Lowell, Joaquin Miller, Archibald MacLeish, Charles Reznikoff, Wallace Stevens and John Godfrey Saxe."); *Sidney Lanier and the Poetry of Legal Morality*, 25 Cumb. L. Rev. 309 (1995); and *William Cullen Bryant and the Poetry of Natural Law*, 30 Akron L. Rev. 661 (1997).

Steven Richman is a Princeton, New Jersey, lawyer, poet, and photographer. He obtained his law degree from New York University School of Law in 1980. Richman practices national and international commercial law, including trademark and copyright law, business torts, and contract law. Richman is the author of four photography books and a collection of poetry, *Mixed Exits*, published by the *Legal Studies Forum* in 2012.

18 Law and Literature, in one disguise or another, has existed in the United States from the earliest days of

the republic. Lawyers, as we first learn from our European ancestors, have always had a close association with literature. Lawyers, in this close association with literature, were once educated to become members of a *learned profession*, and even today, in a time when the legal profession is more instrumental in its orientation, lawyers continue to find a way to use literature in their work. Lawyers have, as we know, always been poets and novelists, journalists and historians; lawyers have been involved in these endeavors throughout the history of the United States.

The conventional view today is that Law and Literature is a "movement" in legal scholarly circles, and that this movement emerged in the 1970s and 1980s and became a school of contemporary jurisprudence. For those holding this conventional view—that Law and Literature is a 1970s phenomenon—there is frequent reference to James Boyd White and his publication of *The Legal Imagination: Studies in the Nature of Legal Thought and Expression* (Little, Brown & Co., 1973) as the seminal event in the emergence of the Law and Literature movement. While there is no question about the singular influence of White's *The Legal Imagination* (and his later writings) on the field of Law and Literature, White does not claim to be a founder of the Law and Literature movement, and he has shown no great enthusiasm to defend or define the movement/discipline parameters of Law and Literature.

I became a law student in 1967; there was no talk about Law and Literature. In the 1960s Law and Literature, had, temporarily, gone underground, and would not emerge into open view until we begin to see clear signs of the demise of law as an autonomous discipline. For my part, the late 1960s was a perfectly wonderful time to begin the study of law; one could feel the jurisprudential ground shift beneath our feet, even though we had no clear-cut labels to describe the reconfigured landscape that would later include: Critical Legal Studies, Feminist Jurisprudence, Law and Literature, Narrative Jurisprudence, Critical Race Theory, and Law and Economics. In the late 1960s, activity along the jurisprudence fault-lines resulted in new schools of "contemporary jurisprudence"; changes in legal scholarship begin to unfold, and along with that unfolding, we had a sense that legal education would begin to undergo a real transformation.

The publication most often identified with the emergence of Law and Literature is James Boyd White's *The Legal Imagination*. And what great fortune to have modern-day Law and Literature re-emerge from such an imaginative text. White did things no other legal scholar had tried to do (and few have done since); he presented Law and Literature as a teaching text rather than still another description of the world of law and lawyers represented in the works of literature. White reminded us of what we attempted to forget: *The world of law and the work of lawyers is a literary enterprise.* In White's *The Legal Imagination*, we were no longer admonished to read great literature that would in some magical way make us great legal advocates. Rather than read "great books," we were encouraged to be more attentive to the language in which we conduct our work, the reading this work entails, and the rhetoric by which we define (and limit) ourselves as lawyers. White presented Law and Literature as a perspective, a way of thinking about ourselves as lawyers. White invited us to engage in the kind of writing and thinking—that is, a way of thinking about writing and getting our thinking into writing—by which we could adopt and adapt literary thinking and literary sensibilities in our work as lawyers.

19 On this new direction in "law and literature" scholarship, and how it might change the focus of our teaching of law and literature in American law schools, *see* William Domnarki, *Law and Literature*, 27 Legal Stud. F. 109 (2003).

20 For John William Corrington's tribute to Southern poetry, *see* John William Corrington, *Lines to the South, and Other Poems* (Louisiana State University Press, 1965) and John William Corrington & Miller Williams (eds.), *Southern Writing in the Sixties: Poetry* (Louisiana State University Press, 1966).

21 Armistead C. Gordon Jr., *Virginia Writers of Fugitive Verse* 3 (James T. White & Co., 1922). Thomas Nelson Page, still another lawyer poet, explains in his introduction to *Virginia Writers of Fugitive Verse* that "fugitive verse" refers to poems that have not been previously "collected" and have not appeared in "volume-form." *Id*. at xiii–xv.

22 Armistead C. Gordon (1855–1931): Armistead Chuchill Gordon was born at Edgeworth, Virginia, in 1855. He became a lawyer, practiced in Staunton, Virginia, and went on to become mayor of that city in 1884, serving two years. He also served as Commonwealth's Attorney. Gordon was a graduate of Virginia University, founded by his grandfather General W. F. Gordon; he received an honorary Doctor

of Divinity degree from Washington and Lee University in 1923. *See* Edmund Clarence Stedman (ed.), *An American Anthology 1787–1899* 795 (Houghton, Mifflin & Co., 1900). Armistead C. Gordon's poetry includes: *For Truth and Freedom: Poems of Commemoration* (A. Shultz, 1898); *The Western Front: A Little Calendar of the Great War* (Privately Printed [Staunton, Virginia], 1928); *The Fount of Castaly* (Historical Pub. Co., 1934).

23 Identifying lawyer poets, engaged in an archaeology of literary history, I began to toy with a thought experiment: I would write a history of the United States told through the lives—the writing—the poetry—of lawyer poets. I consulted Whyte Holt, a legal historian and friend, about the project to learn he thought far less highly of the proposed project than I did. In a sane moment, I realized my proposed history would push my work with lawyer poets into the realm of intellectual folly. The project would have required me to be the historian I am not.

III

seemingly different universes— law & poetry

IMAGINE, IF YOU WILL, Archibald MacLeish, a stately and distinguished man, a graduate of our most elite schools—Hotchkiss, Yale, Harvard Law School—a man whose place in the law could not have been more secure—the good life appeared to be his ordained destiny. There was a partnership in the offering at the Boston law firm Choate, Hall and Stewart, and rumors of a standing offer to join the Harvard Law School faculty. MacLeish walks away from this life—his establishment life—his life as a lawyer—to be a poet who would receive three Pulitzer Prizes for his poetry. While he may have abandoned a promising career as a lawyer—he practiced law for only three years—MacLeish never forgot his Harvard Law School education. And it seems he was never allowed by his lawyer colleagues at Harvard to forget that it was out of the ordinary—odd—for a man to give up law to be a poet.

MacLeish, just weeks after turning eighty, appeared as a guest at the Eighty-Fifth Anniversary Banquet of Editors of the *Harvard Law Review*. In his remarks at the banquet gathering, published under the title "Apologia" in the *Harvard Law Review*, MacLeish doesn't dwell on the parade of events of an accomplished life that followed his abandonment of the legal profession. What MacLeish does is use the occasion to reflect on how in becoming a poet he made himself a strange bird in the eyes of his Harvard colleagues.[1] MacLeish, in his banquet remarks, describes himself as "a Law Review dropout, a maker of verses, a fifth intellectual wheel, a dispensable irrelevance." The great irony in MacLeish's self-description is that he lived, as well as a man can, a life in opposition to irrelevance, a life that undermines the idea that a poet cannot be involved in the affairs of the world. MacLeish was an avowedly public man, evidenced in his writings and his service in governmental and diplomatic positions. MacLeish's passion for poetry may have taken him away from the practice of law, but it never isolated him from the social and political world he inhabited.

In his "Apologia," MacLeish seems compelled—driven—to deal with the conventional notion that lawyers and poets exist in different universes. The conventional truth seems to be: follow law and betray the Muse, give up law to follow and befriend the Muse. The Muse turns out to be no less the jealous mistress than law.[2]

MacLeish struggled with this conventional thinking about lawyers and poets, and had wrestled fitfully to arrive at the decision to abandon the legal profession. In his presentation to the *Harvard Law Review* editors at their banquet gathering, MacLeish appears to have in mind a return to the scene of his "crime." This is the way MacLeish describes the "two worlds" problem in his presentation at the Harvard Law Review editors banquet:

> The fundamental assumption, common to all these pleasant occasions, seem[s] to be that although a *Law Review* editor might reasonably be expected to end up as president of a bank or head of the Natural Gas Association, he ha[s] no right to turn himself into a poet. Why? I don't know, though I have often asked. People shuffle their feet and light a cigarette and look away and you walk back to the [Harvard] Yard wondering if you really are queer after all.

MacLeish concludes that those who think him odd must assume there "to be a difference in nature, a difference in worlds [between law and poetry], a difference so fundamental that it reflected in some way on the [Harvard Law] School itself" when he made the decision to pursue poetry. It is a way of thinking that MacLeish feels compelled to address. For those who have so seamlessly bound their lives to the law and to all it represents, thinking about any other life seems to provoke a moment of uneasiness (acting as if they are being asked to undertake a perilous mountain passage).³

MacLeish tries to burrow into this conventional thinking about law and poetry by taking account of being thought odd by fellow Harvard lawyers who could not imagine choosing poetry over law. MacLeish admits there are some rather obvious differences between endeavors undertaken in the name of law and poetry. But with the obvious declared, MacLeish posits this question: "[I]s the difference between the law as the [Harvard Law] School teaches it and poetry as a man pursues it as deep and wide as all that?" Whatever it is that poets do, or lawyers may think poets do, MacLeish lays claim to the proposition that "this does not mean that poets exist in a world of their own or even that they cannot live and breathe in the lawyer's world."

Lawyers and poets may do different things in their day-to-day work, but MacLeish, with the hindsight of his time practicing law and having made his way to become a full-fledged citizen of the poetry world, imagines a bridge between the realms of law and poetry—two grand kingdoms—old kingdoms—each with its own sovereign existence. The bridge MacLeish presents to attendees at the Harvard Law Review banquet is constructed from what he sees as the mutually shared purposes served by poetry and by law. "The business of the law," MacLeish tells us, "is to make sense of the confusion of what we call human life—to reduce it to order but at the same time to give it possibility, scope, even dignity." And the business of poetry? "Precisely to make sense of the chaos of our lives. To create the understanding of our lives. To compose an order which the bewildered, angry heart can recognize. To imagine man."

MacLeish concludes his *Harvard Law Review* banquet remarks by reminding the audience of his settled conviction that in all his endeavors it was the *education* he received at the Harvard Law School that mattered most:

> And what was the substance of that education? The Socratic spark which set insatiable fires where no flame was ever seen before—and not in my mind only but in many others (I think of my classmate at Yale and in the School—my late and oldest friend, Dean Acheson). But beyond the spark? Beyond the spark a vision—the vision of mental time, of the interminable journey of the human mind, the great tradition of the intellectual past which knows the

bearings of the future. No one, not the most erudite or scholarly man, who has failed to see that vision can truly serve the art of poetry or any other art, and by no study better than the study of the law can that great sight be seen. The law has one way of seeing it. Poetry has another. But the journey is the same.

MacLeish's *Harvard Law Review* "apologia" provides an opportunity to confront the conventional expectation that lawyers and poets adopt well-defined "roles" and "images" that fit their place in compartmentalized worlds—one world for law—another world for poetry. The problem is that lawyer and poet stereotypes tell no more than half the story. Tim Nolan, who has written about his own practice of law and poetry, reminds us that stereotypes that lend themselves to mental efficiency, may "fall apart when applied to a single human being. The mask of the poet or mask of the lawyer are poor substitutes for the real human being and his collection of fear, joy, bewilderment and experience."[4]

Archibald MacLeish finds it of some significance—in the august company of *Harvard Law Review* editors—to make clear that he is a poet who has returned home to honor his education as a lawyer. There would be no oddness of the kind acknowledged by MacLeish if Harvard Law School could make way for its graduates to understand that the practice of law—a life in law—can be enhanced by the poet's sensibilities, introspection, awareness, and attentive use of language. If we think literature matters, matters in some continuing way in sustaining belief that our use and regard for language drives toward a worthwhile future, then the best education of a lawyer remains an education in skills practiced by poets. (What we need, one might think, is a poetics-inspired awareness of our legal endeavors.)

A New York lawyer, Daniel F. Tritter, observes that in his trial practice the contemplation of literary matters is never far from his thinking. He goes on to muse:

> Perhaps law educators now [with the emergence of "law and literature" as a development in contemporary jurisprudence and legal scholarship] see an opportunity to rescue the profession from creeping tedium. Does this portend a new kind of lawyer to be minted for the new millennium? For those of us who have never stopped dreaming of a civilized profession, where the word is its enduring currency, we wish it so.[5]

The "new kind of lawyer" envisioned by Daniel Tritter is not really "new." We have *always* had lawyer poets; we still do. Should we be surprised to learn that lawyers, by training, grounded in craft skills attuned to the nuance of language, schooled in the clever rhetorical use of language, studious performers in high legal dramas of our time (in and out of the courtroom), become poets? Accustomed as we may be in this John Grisham era of legal thrillers to a generation of lawyer novelists, there is still some mystery, wonderment, bedevilment at the idea of a person who has the capacity and sensibilities, skills and talents, to be an accomplished poet and a practicing lawyer. Lawyer poets are the iconoclasts of our time.

■

Wallace Stevens, in his early seventies, was invited by Morris Peckham, director of an institute for training young executives at the University of Pennsylvania, to address the institute's graduating trainees on being an insurance company executive and a poet. Declining the invitation, Stevens noted: "I have never believed that it took a great deal to be both a poet and something else, and to lend myself to the opposite belief, as if to illustrate it and even expound it, would be difficult."[6]

Stevens, unlike MacLeish, seems never to have found it odd that he was an insurance company lawyer and a poet, and that being engaged in law and poetry, being acclaimed in the poetry world, was anything to be considered exceptional. In a letter to Harvey Breit, written over a decade before the letter to Peckham, Stevens asks: "After all, what is there odd about being a lawyer and being or doing something else at the same time?" As Stevens put it, in a follow-up letter to Breit, two days later: "I don't have a separate mind for legal work and another for writing poetry. I do each with my whole mind . . . ." Simply put, for Stevens, "one is not a lawyer one minute and a poet the next." Stevens declined Breit's invitation to be interviewed and photographed for a *Harper's Bazaar* article that would focus on his being a lawyer and a poet; he suggested that if Breit wanted to pursue this idea that law and poetry endeavors exist in opposition, then he might contact Archibald MacLeish or Edgar Lee Masters. Stevens, writing to Harvey Breit, who had been commissioned to do the article, pointed out that the "real subject" of his article might be "destroying the caricature in people's minds that exists there as the image of the poet." Stevens goes on to suggest: "If we could get rid of all the caricatures of the past: the caricatures not only of the poet . . . but also the caricatures of the business man and the barkeeper and of a lot of other people, we should only be seeing what we see every day, which is not so easy after all." Stevens sought to live a life that called for and allowed him to see beyond caricatures.⁷

Stevens was memorialized after his death by Archibald MacLeish in a poem MacLeish recites for his audience at the gathering of *Harvard Law Review* editors. The poem, "Reasons for Music," reads in part:

> The labor of order has no rest:
> To impose on the confused, fortuitous
>
> Flowing away of the world, Form—
> Still, cold, clean, obdurate,
>
> Lasting forever, or at least
> Lasting . . . .⁸

One may find it odd, given MacLeish's audience, and having later published his remarks in the *Harvard Law Review*, that he would fail to mention (at least in the published version of his remarks) that Stevens was a fellow lawyer (and had attended Harvard for several years of his undergraduate work).

Stevens avoided, as best he could, efforts to make his work as surety/bond/guaranty lawyer (and corporate executive) at the Hartford Accident and Indemnity Insurance Company and being, at the same time, an acclaimed poet appear to be anything unusual or extraordinary in any way. Others clearly found Stevens's situation an oddity—that Stevens found no reason to address. Stevens, often identified as an insurance executive, seemed to have always identified himself as a lawyer. Stevens, writing to Victor Hammer, noted: "While I am in the insurance business, I am a lawyer and all my work is on the legal side."

Chapter III
Endnotes

1 Archibald MacLeish's "Apologia," appeared in 85 Harv. L. Rev. 1505 (1972). MacLeish included the apologia in a collection of essays and commentaries, *Riders on the Earth*, where he (or his editor) retitled his "Apologia" with the more generic-sounding "Art and Law." Archibald MacLeish, *Riders on the Earth: Essays and Recollections* 82–88 (Houghton Mifflin, 1978). Reviewing the various meanings and root of the term *apologia*—relying on my dictionary of choice, *Webster's Seventh New Collegiate Dictionary*—suggests that MacLeish seems to have found a title befitting his remarks, a title, considering MacLeish's academic and literary background, that was undoubtedly carefully chosen. One suspects that Archibald MacLeish was, in his apologia, working out for himself, in his presentation to an audience of lawyers, an accounting of how he has lived in two worlds, worlds of the kind we imagine to be something like sovereign universes.

MacLeish's first book of poetry appeared in 1917 while he was serving in the Army, his wartime service interrupting his studies at Harvard Law School. MacLeish finished his law studies after the war, practiced law with the Boston firm Choate, Hall and Stewart for three years, and after a protracted struggle with himself, gave up the practice of law to become a poet. In addition to his poetry, MacLeish was a dramatist, statesman, and diplomat. He published twenty-one books of poetry, seventeen volumes of drama (many of them in verse), and another seventeen books of prose (political writings and essays, including two books of essays on poetry).One of MacLeish's Pulitzer Prizes came for his epic poem *Conquistador* (Houghton Mifflin Co., 1932), which he researched by retracing the route of Cortez's army through Mexico. A second Pulitzer came in 1952 for his *Collected Poems 1917–1952* (Houghton Mifflin Co., 1952), while the third Pulitzer was for *J. B.* (Houghton Mifflin Co., 1957), a drama in verse.

MacLeish returned to Harvard as the Boylston Professor of Rhetoric and Oratory in 1949 and remained until 1962 when he reached the age for mandatory retirement.

2 We know that law can be a jealous mistress in its dominating ways in the life of a lawyer, and in the life of a culture. Poetry has no great impulse to dominate, yet steadfastly insists on having a seat at the table where the great feast is being served. Poetry seems forever to be in danger of being left out in the cold. Wallace Stevens noted once that, "a man who writes poetry never really gets away from it. He may not continue to write it as poetry, but he always remains a poet in one form or another." Wallace Stevens's letter to Thomas McGreevy, dated April 20, 1948, in Holly Stevens (ed.), *Letters of Wallace Stevens* 586 (University of California Press, 1996). The imminently quotable Ralph Waldo Emerson observed that "Art is a jealous mistress, and, if a man has a genius for painting, poetry, music, architecture or philosophy, he makes a bad husband and an ill provider . . . ." Ralph Waldo Emerson, *The*

Conduct of Life 112 (Riverside Press, new & revised ed., 1883) (vol. 6, Emerson's Complete Works).

Reading the poetry of lawyers, we find that few lawyers look to their poetry to tell us anything about law and what it means to inhabit a world of lawyers. Few lawyers, serious about being poets, make either law or legal practice a theme of their poetry. Poetry takes the lawyer beyond law, just as readers of poetry we get beyond the boxes in which the world (and law) seek to confine us.

3   For an account of one memorable mountain passage, see Bowen H. McCoy, *The Parable of the Sadhu*, 75 (3) Harv. Bus. Rev. 54 (1997).

4   Tim Nolan, *Poetry and the Practice of Law*, 46 S.D. L. Rev. 677, 686 (2001). Nolan observes that we think of the poet as "bohemian, irresponsible, free, flighty, subject to brilliant inspiration, aloof, poor, garrotted, soulful, irrelevant." The stereotypical image of the lawyer is "masterful, composed, certain, needling, dogged, practical, insistent, combative, annoying, overdressed." *Id.* at 685. Keep in mind, that we are dealing here with stereotypes, and as damning and pernicious as they can be, they also, as Nolan points out, "serve a purpose." We use stereotypes in our thinking because they are efficient, lead us astray as they so often do, pernicious as they can become. Nolan reminds us that stereotypes "calm the mind and reassure a person that he knows what he does not know." *Id.*

For still another view of the stereotypes that follow lawyers and poets, and the MacLeish effort to imagine a bridge between law and poetry, consider this effort to describe the stereotypes:

To the literary man, the language of the law is likely to seem abstract, cumbersome, and remote from life, though alarmingly powerful over the actions of human beings. On the other hand, the legal man, who often believes himself sympathetic to books and the arts, thinks of literary study nevertheless as irrelevant to his own profession, fuzzy in its definitions, and essentially a frivolous "escape." Both these judgments are more than half wrong. The two worlds of discourse are certainly different, and should be, but they may have something to learn from one another, and an effort to open communications might actually provide some useful consequences for both parties.

Walker Gibson, *Literary Minds and Judicial Style*, 6 Scribes J. Legal Writing 115 (1996–1997) [reprinted from 36 N.Y.U. L. Rev. 915 (1961)].

Timothy Nolan (1954–   ) was born in Minneapolis, Minnesota. He graduated from the University of Minnesota in 1978 with a B.A. in English. He and his wife, Kate, moved to New York City in 1978 where he obtained an M.F.A. degree in writing from Columbia University, worked as an archivist at the Whitney Museum, and read the poetry slush pile for Paris Review. He returned to Minnesota in 1985 and received his J.D. degree from William Mitchell College of Law in 1989. Nolan's published poetry includes: *The Sound of It* (New Rivers Press, 2008); *And Then* (New Rivers Press, 2012); *The Field* (New Rivers Press, 2016); and *Lines: Poems* (Nodin Press, 2022).

5   Daniel F. Tritter, *Lusty Voice II*, 10 Cardozo Stud. L. & Literature 143 (1998). "To study this legacy [of

law in the early days of American literature and the literary aspirations of early lawyers] is," Robert Ferguson reminds us, a way to retain the legacy of the literary lawyer "for a modern culture in which the stark separation of intellect, art, and politics should give every citizen pause." Robert A. Ferguson, *Law and Letters in American Culture* 10 (Harvard University Press, 1984).

6   Wallace Stevens letter to Morris Peckham, dated January 19, 1954, in Holly Stevens (ed.), *Letters of Wallace Stevens* 814–815 (University of California Press, 96, 1966). Additional references to Stevens's commentary in his letters cited in the text are: Stevens's letter to Morris Peckham, dated January 19, 1954, at 814–815; Stevens's letter to Harvey Breit, dated July 29, 1942, at 413–415; Stevens's July 27, 1942, letter to Breit, at 413; Stevens's letter to Breit, dated July 29, 1942; Stevens's letter to Victor Hammer, dated July 20, 1948, at 606–607.

7   Lawyers and poets tend, within their own camps, to think rather grandly of themselves, and in doing so, embrace some elements of the stereotypes that help bolster their image and deny elements of stereotypes that make them look bad. This business of celebration and damnation of lawyers and poets becomes rather confused when we find a man or woman embracing the practices of both lawyer and poet. Whatever one may think of lawyers and poets, we are fast becoming a society in which we know far more about lawyers than we do poets. We know it to be the exceptional reader and person who reads and sets his compass by poetry. With our great ignorance if not active disdain of poetry, how can

the poet be anything other than a stereotype (or a mythical construct)?

8 MacLeish's Wallace Stevens poem, "Reasons for Music," appears in Archibald MacLeish, *Songs for Eve* 57–58 (Houghton Mifflin/Riverside Press, 1954). ("Reasons for Music" is the final poem in the collection.)

IV

talking to lawyers about their poetry

IT WAS THE GHOST-LIKE PRESENCE of old lawyer poets that prompted me to turn my attention to contemporary lawyer poets. I had a sense I might learn something about their life—and my own—if I could understand how they navigated the seemingly diverse worlds of law and poetry. To my surprise, my effort to converse with lawyer poets was far more difficult than I anticipated. Frankly, many of the first conversations I initiated were awkward. My curiosity about what I saw as a life lived in "two worlds" took the conversation nowhere. I was constantly reminded of Wallace Stevens's avoidance of the idea that lawyer poets live in "two worlds"—for Wallace Stevens there was no two worlds.

I began to detect a pattern in these awkward conversations: I would introduce myself by explaining how I had been teaching "lawyers and literature" for several decades and in the course of my teaching had become intrigued by lawyers who have become poets (and poets, like John William Corrington, who become lawyers). I explained my historical literary research—the effort to identify lawyer poets throughout our history.[1] Variations of these introductory remarks didn't seem to improve the situation—time after time, conversations faltered. Nothing seemed to work. Obviously something wasn't right. I began to realize that the hesitancy I experienced in these conversations came from the fact that I was taking the conversation in one direction when the lawyers with whom I was talking had in mind taking it in a different direction. Of more interest to the lawyers than anything I was saying about lawyers and poets navigating two worlds, was the question—*How did you find me and my poetry?* When the question was posed, I tried to use it as an invitation to elaborate on how I placed lawyer poets work in the context of the "law and literature" movement. The lawyers, courteous to a fault, would hear me out, but not being academics, had far less interest in the "law and literature" movement than I did. The point was clear: to converse with lawyer poets I would need to find something to talk about that would sustain the conversation.

Along the way, I had a few lawyers ask me directly: *Have you read my poetry?* (or some disguised version of the question). It took some time to hear what was being implied in the *have you read my poetry* question. I finally began to see what the poet was saying: *If you haven't read my poetry, we have little to talk about that is of immediate interest to me.* When I initiated these conversations, I assumed we had mutual interest and something to talk about. Lawyers seem to share that view only when I could confirm I had read their poetry. I began to see the poet's point: *You have discovered I am a poet and taken the initiative to begin this conversation. So, let's talk about poetry.* I could not escape the logic: Of more interest than the historical lawyer poets I was identifying, that lawyer poets have a place in the "law and literature" movement, is the poetry now being written by lawyers. Simply put: Our conversation depended on a *reading of the poetry*. It would have sounded preposterous to admit: *I have set out to identify lawyer poets and figure out what it might mean to engage in these rather diverse endeavors but I have no interest in the poetry written by lawyers.*

What followed was another observation: Simply reading the poetry would not suffice. *I must have something to say about what I read.* Obviously, I can't call a lawyer to say, "I have found you and your poetry. I read your poetry and find I have nothing to say about it." Or still more perverse: "I have read your poetry and, frankly, I don't much care for it." The only conversation that makes sense, a conversation of interest to both the poet and to myself, is a conversation about poetry that in some way or another intrigues me (poetry I value enough to read well enough to discuss).

So begins a new daily practice—*reading poetry*. I read poetry so I can talk to lawyers who have found a way to live in two worlds—law and poetry (or like Wallace Stevens, live a life in which the two worlds is not an existential concern). To talk to lawyers about the two worlds problem, or anything else, I found it necessary to read their poetry and have something to say about it. Lawyers, learning that I had sought out their poetry—read it—seemed to think we had something to talk about.[2]

■

Two years before these conversations with lawyer poets got underway, I had taken on editorship of the *Legal Studies Forum*, an eclectic transdisciplinary journal that survived an improbable founding in the 1970s by the faculty of an undergraduate legal studies program at the University of Massachusetts–Amherst.[3] If there is anything odder—more obsessive—than trying to identify America's lawyer poets, it is editing a journal for twenty-four years. A journal takes over an editor's life like invasive bamboo. With the identification of lawyer poets—eventually several thousand in number—the lawyer poets project takes still a new turn: I decide to publish the poetry of lawyers in the *Legal Studies Forum*.

In 1996, when I became editor of *LSF,* the journal had already published some of the early "law and literature" writings in the late 1970s and early 1980s at a time when the field of "law and literature" was first emerging. When I assumed editorship of *LSF*, I began to give the journal a literary focus, a move that opened the door to publishing the poetry of lawyers. *LSF* had, before the emergence of the lawyer poets project, published issues that featured "legal fiction," most notably, stories by Lowell Komie (in an *LSF* issue in 2001) and John William Corrington (in a 2002 issue).[4] I must say, I didn't see anything out of the ordinary in the idea of publishing poetry composed by lawyers. I had discovered, sailing uncharted waters, some rather intriguing poetry that happened to be written by lawyers. What seemed obvious at the time was that lawyer poets represent a relatively unexplored dimension of the field of "law and literature." What followed, was an assumption (perhaps a peculiar one): *Poetry written by lawyers might be of interest in the world of lawyers simply because it is the work of colleagues who have undertaken a genre of writing so many of us know so little about (a genre some of us find exotic). Reading this poetry of lawyers—whatever our initial purpose for this reading may be—we end up reading poetry that provides its own purpose for reading.* If your neighbor published a novel, wouldn't you be curious and want to read it? If you found the neighbor's novel intriguing, wouldn't you seek the fictional work of other neighbors whom you could identify as novelists?

■

It was 2003. I rounded up a small group of lawyer poets in the United States, among them, T. S. Kerrigan, Lillian Baker Kennedy, Helen Bailey, Daniel M. Caine, and Stan Biderman, and a Canadian lawyer, Gary Botting, and convinced them—with full disclosure of my novice status as a reader of poetry—to allow me to publish some thirty-seven poems (comprising fifty-four pages) in *LSF*.[5] The presentation of the poems was—how best to describe it—rough. The result was most definitely not a typographical triumph. My inexperience in working with the printer to get the right layout of the poems was evident. The poets were forgiving; no one made a fuss about this questionable first effort to publish poetry in *LSF*. It was a start. I had to think the kinks would get worked out in future efforts.

In 2003, after publishing several issues featuring the work of John William Corrington the previous year and the lackluster first effort in publishing poetry, I devoted a substantial part of an *LSF* issue to John William Corrington's poetry and an edited selection of Corrington's correspondence with the poet Charles Bukowski.[6] This time, we finally got the poetry to look right on the page. I was pleased with the new layout.

Engaged in a supportive correspondence with T. S. Kerrigan, one of the first lawyer poets I published in 2003, I began to look critically at the work of contemporary lawyer poets for a poetry anthology issue of *LSF*. I couldn't find any evidence that anyone else had attempted such an anthology; *LSF* would make it happen.

Yes, I was finding the occasional poem related to the practice of law, but the poems that most intrigued me, the poems I experienced the most pleasure in reading, were poems where the lawyer was not using the poems to tell us anything about the world of law and lawyering but was simply being a poet.[7] Surrounded by a growing library of poetry—all by practicing lawyers or former lawyers—I began to assemble an anthology of poetry comprised of poems written by lawyers. In February 2004, the *Legal Studies Forum* published *Off the Record: An Anthology of Poetry by Lawyers* featuring the work of sixty-six lawyer poets and 679 pages of their poetry—the first anthology of non-law-related poetry of lawyers ever published.[8]

■

Off the Record received an enthusiastic response. Several of the lawyers whose poetry appeared in the anthology voiced surprise that so many fellow lawyers were poets, and floated the idea of a gathering of lawyer poets to celebrate the publication of the new *LSF* anthology. With the first anthology of non-law-related poetry of lawyers in hand, a celebration of some sort seemed to be in order. For various reasons (too mundane to enumerate), I did not follow up on the idea. A decision I now regret. Carl Reisman, an Urbana, Illinois, lawyer and poet took an interest in the idea and refused to let my reluctance deter him from finding folks at the law school at the University of Illinois who were willing to support the gathering (that would, in the way of academics, end up being called a "conference"). I agreed to work with Carl to help organize the gathering and invite a selection of poets whose work had appeared in the *LSF* anthology to make presentations at the conference. Carl, to my surprise, got the University of Illinois folks to approve a final proposal and things began to fall into place. The conference, held in February 2007, was accurately billed as the first conference of its kind. Unfortunately, the conference, instead of being presented as a celebration of lawyers who write poetry was described as a conference "to explore and celebrate the relationship between law and poetry."

I was eager to attend the conference and give the opening presentation. A day before my planned departure for the conference, a massive winter snowstorm descended on north-central West Virginia. If, by some miraculous effort, I had actually managed to get to the airport, it was clear my flight to Chicago would be canceled. The first ever gathering of lawyer poets—the first that any of us had any knowledge—I would miss it. Carl worked diligently to find a way to get me to Urbana, and I felt quite miserable to miss a celebration of work I had set in motion. To miss another conference was no great loss; to miss the celebration that Carl Reisman had organized left me out of sorts and more than a little sad.

With a major winter storm preventing me from joining Carl Reisman at the gathering of lawyer poets in Urbana, Illinois, Carl insisted that I prepare remarks that he could pass along, in some form, to those who would brave the winter storm to attend the conference.

■

I deeply regret that a winter storm keeps me in West Virginia when I most want to be in Urbana with lawyers whose poetry I have come to admire, poetry to which I have devoted my attention in recent years.

I want to warmly thank the Dean and faculty at the University of Illinois College of Law and the University of Illinois Master of Fine Arts Creative Writing Program who are jointly hosting the conference. And, I extend my warmest personal thanks and eternal gratitude to Carl Reisman, a lawyer, a poet, and a wonderful colleague who took the initiative and made this conference a reality. If Carl had had his way, and a Learjet, I'd be present with you this evening instead of sending these remarks from a far distance!

If there is any good fortune in being stranded in West Virginia, it means you will be spared a lecture—a lecture in which I would have tried to inflame your imagination with tales of the glorious (and sometimes not so glorious) history of lawyer poets in America. That history, so far as I can determine, begins with the arrival in Massachusetts of the scandal-prone Thomas Morton in 1624. I had the gnawing, uneasy suspicion that my history of lawyer poets in America lecture would be more than adequate to put a room filled with hardy winter souls to sleep. Yes, I think it's true that Thomas Morton was one of our first lawyer poets, and as it would happen, he was something of a scoundrel. Given the legal situation in the colonies, it seems unlikely that Thomas Morton was ever to do much in the way of anything we would associate with the practice of law in his adopted "new land." Even so, I'm confident that Thomas Morton's exploits as colonist renegade and poet would not have been sufficient to keep you awake, even if I could have made headway in arguing the case that Morton was the first lawyer poet in America.

When Carl insisted I send some remarks, I fully abandoned the idea of a lecture on the history of lawyer poets in America. In lieu of a lecture, I want to tell a story—a "teacher's tale"—about how my work with lawyer poets got underway and how I was a most unlikely person to be doing any kind of academic work that would involve poetry. I can't promise you that my teacher's tale will be sufficient justification for your efforts to brave the weather to be present for this gathering of lawyer poets. A cliché comes to mind: Hope springs eternal.

My story begins with an admission: My work with poetry, and with the lawyers who write it, has been an improbable venture. In the millennium summer of 2000, the Y2K scare beginning to recede in the rearview mirror, I set out to write about a lawyer—novelist—poet—screenwriter—philosopher—bass fisherman named John William Corrington (a writer I would be surprised to learn anyone at this conference had ever heard of). With the idea of writing about Corrington—a rather intriguing figure—I found myself coming around, again and again, to an aspect of Corrington's life that made him, for me, such an enigma: He was a poet who became a lawyer, only to abandon the legal profession to spend the remainder of his life as a writer. What I had most trouble getting my head around—an oddness if you will—at least what I found at the time to be odd—was a man being a lawyer and a poet. This oddness, it seems quite clear, is anchored in stereotypes of the sort I suspect many lawyers and non-lawyers alike hold, hold in a way that channels our thinking about who poets are and who lawyers are and how they are so radically different.

You know the stereotypes. We all do. It was an effort to address, and to confront these stereotypes that inform and distort our thinking, that prompted my curiosity about John William Corrington. When I started the Corrington work, I knew of exactly two lawyer poets: Wallace Stevens and Archibald MacLeish. My friend Lowell Komie, a Chicago lawyer and writer, when I told him of my interest in lawyer poets, informed me that he knew of two: Edgar Lee Masters and Charles Reznikoff. I might have done well to let the list of lawyer poets lie with the four—Wallace Stevens, Archibald MacLeish, Edgar Lee Masters, and Charles Reznikoff. I had four major figures I could study, four that would provide me with something—I had no idea what—to say about Corrington's endeavors as a poet and lawyer. I might be able to sketch out something to say about stereotypes of lawyer and poet and how the lawyer poet finds a way to defy (or reinforce) our stereotypes. For reasons that lie well beyond the horizon of understanding, I didn't stop with the four lawyer poets. If there is anything to be said for an "irresistible impulse," anything to the notion that we are sometimes called to do things for which we have no ready explanation, that we sometimes eagerly set out on forays for which we have no maps and no guides, my efforts to identify lawyer poets ranks among the impulses I found irresistible.

I think it fair to say I had no clear-cut reason to take up with lawyer poets, in part because I am not, I would readily admit, a poet. I wasn't in search of lawyer poets to be among my own kind or to justify an interest in poetry. Indeed, when I began to identify the lawyer poets, having no affinity for poetry, I didn't give the first thought to the idea that the historical work in identifying lawyer poets had anything remotely related to do with reading poetry. Doing historical literary research is one thing; reading poetry is quite another!

Chapter IV
Endnotes

1. The lawyer poets I identified in my historical research is set forth in the Appendix: A Chronological Index of Lawyer Poets.
2. Several years after the lawyer poets project got underway, I published conversations with three lawyer poets: T. S. Kerrigan, Simon Perchik, and Ruthann Robson.

Tom Kerrigan
31 Legal Stud. F. 473 (2007)

T. S. Kerrigan was born in 1939 in Los Angeles. He attended the University of California, Berkeley, and received his law degree from Loyola University in Los Angeles. Kerrigan's poetry has appeared in various periodicals, both in the United States and in Europe, including: *Southern Review*, *International Poetry Review*, *Poetry Monthly*, *Kansas Quarterly*, *Pacific Review*, and *Tennessee Quarterly*. Kerrigan's *Another Bloomsday at Molly Malone's Pub*, a collection of poetry, was published by Inevitable Press in 1999. Kerrigan's poetry also includes: *The Shadow Sonnets and Other Poems* (Scienter Press, 2006) and *My Dark People* (Central Avenue Press, 2008). Kerrigan's work has been anthologized in Garrison Keillor's *Good Poems*, published by Viking/Penguin in 2002. Kerrigan is not only a poet, but a playwright. He is the author of "Branches Among the Stars" (Louisville, 1990). His plays have been produced in Los Angeles at the Ensemble Studio Theatre (where he formerly served as a member of the Board of

Directors) and at the Globe Playhouse. Kerrigan has also been a theater critic and a member of the Los Angeles Drama Critics' Circle, and he participated in the UCLA National Playwrights Conference. Kerrigan, past president of the Irish American Bar Association, in 2001 argued Lujan v. G&G Fire Sprinklers, Inc. in the U.S. Supreme Court, and won the case decisively. *See* T. S. Kerrigan, *Before the Supreme Court*, 27 Legal Stud. F. 277 (2003).

Simon Perchik
29 Legal Stud. F. 181 (2005)

Simon Perchik (1923–2022) was born in 1923 in Paterson, New Jersey. He is a graduate of New York University where he received both his B.A. in English and his law degree. Perchik was a pilot during World War II and awarded the Distinguished Flying Cross, Air Medal with three Oak Leaf Clusters, ETO Ribbon with three Battle Stars, and the Presidential Unit Citation. He was admitted to the New York Bar in 1951 and was in a private law practice until 1975. He served for five years as assistant district attorney for Suffolk County, New York. Perchik's poetry has, reputedly, appeared in more journals and magazines than any other poet in America.

Perchik's published poetry includes: *I Counted Only April* (Elizabeth Press, 1964); *Twenty Years of Hands* (Elizabeth Press, 1966); *Which Hand Holds the Brother* (Elizabeth Press, 1969); *Hands You Are Secretly Wearing* (Elizabeth Press, 1972); and *Both Hands Screaming* (Elizabeth Press, 1975) (printed in Italy by Stamperia Valdonega); *The Club Fits Either Hand* (Elizabeth Press, 1979); *Mr. Lucky: Poems* (Shearsman Books, 1984); *The Snowcat Poems*

1980–81, to the Photographs of Robert Frank (Linwood Publishers, 1984); *Who Can Touch These Knots: New and Selected Poems* (Scarecrow Press, 1985); *The Gandolf Poems* (White Pine Press, 1988); *I Want My Music Bent* (James L. Weil, [1989]); *Redeeming the Wings* (Dusty Dog Press, 1991); *Birthmark* (Flockophobic Press, 1992); *The Emptiness Between My Hands* (Dusty Dog Press, 1993); *Letters to the Dead* (St. Andrews College Press, 1993); *14 New Poems* (Shearsman Books, 1994); *Shearsman 19* (Shearsman Books, 1994); *These Hands Filled with Numbness* (Dusty Dog Press, 1996); *Touching the Headstone* (Stride Publications, 2000); *Hands Collected 1949–1999* (Pavement Saw Press, 2000); *The Autochthon Poems* (Split Shift Book, 2001); *The Milton Poems* (Ahadada Books Chapbook, 2006); *Rafts* (Parisfel Editions, 2007); *Greatest Hits 1964–2008* (Pudding House Publications, 2009); *Almost Rain* (River Otter Press, 2013); *Fourteen Poems* (CreateSpace, 2015); *The B Poems* (Poets Wear Prada, 2016); and *The Osiris Poems* (Boxofchalk/Forge, 2017). Perchik's final collections of poems in the last years of his life were published by Cholla Needles & Literary Journal [Press]: *The Gibson Poems* (2019); *The Rosenblum Poems* (2019); *Paper The Sun* (2020); *The Weston Poems* (2020); *Peel The Sun* (2021); *Dreams I've Held 1943–1979* (2021); *The Family of Man Poems* (2021); and *The Elliot Erwitt Poems* (2022).

Ruthann Robson
29 Legal Stud. F. 145 (2005)

For my commentary on Robson's writing and our mutual interest in "law and literature," *see* James R.

Elkins, *A Poetics—of and for—Ruthann Robson*, 8 N.Y. City L. Rev. 363 (2005). For Robson's single collection of poems, *see* Ruthann Robson, *Masks* (Leapfrog Press, 1999) (a selection of Robson's poems appears in 29 Legal Stud. F. 95–143 (2005)).

3 The *Legal Studies Forum*, from its founding at the Department of Legal Studies at the University of Massachusetts–Amherst in 1976, where it first served as the newsletter of the American Legal Studies Association (now defunct), staked its claim on being a journal devoted to humanistic, critical, and interdisciplinary approaches to law and legal studies. The humanistic legal education movement, the emergence of Critical Legal Studies, the re-emergence of law and literature, and the flourishing of interdisciplinary legal-studies scholarship were parallel developments with the founding of the *Legal Studies Forum*. My colleagues at the University of Massachusetts–Amherst had a prophetic sense of where legal scholarship was going and where it needed to go.

On the University of Massachusetts–Amherst legal studies program, where *LSF* was founded, *see* Peter d'Errico et al., *Humanistic Legal Studies at the University of Massachusetts at Amherst*, 28 J. Legal Educ. 18 (1976). The *Legal Studies Forum* managed to outlive the American Legal Studies Association, the organization that first published the journal as an organizational newsletter, and continued publication for over four decades. The *Legal Studies Forum* ceased publication in 2020.

4 James R. Elkins (ed.), *The Legal Fiction of Lowell B. Komie*, 25 Legal Stud. F. 1–246 (2001); James R.

Elkins (ed.), *Fiction by John William Corrington*, 26 Legal Stud. F. 1–492 (2002).

In 2002, when I edited and published two issues of the *Legal Studies Forum* devoted to the work of John William Corrington, I did not include Corrington's poetry. I had learned enough as an editor to respect my novice status as a typographer; publishing a poem properly positioned on the page turns out to be substantially more difficult than layout of prose text. I thought too highly of Corrington's work to create a visual mess with his poems.

5   27 Legal Stud. F. 283–345 (2003).

6   For permission to publish the Corrington–Bukowski correspondence, Bill Corrington's poetry, and previous 2002 *LSF* issues devoted to Corrington, I am eternally grateful to Bill Corrington's wife, and collaborator, Joyce Corrington. Joyce provided unwavering support of my efforts to publish her husband's work. In the publication of the Corrington poetry, I began to shore up my wobbly first efforts to see the poetry of lawyers into print.

7   A decade after I published the first poetry in the *Legal Studies Forum*, I reassessed the lawyer-related poetry that appeared in *LSF* over the years and began to see the possibilities for a lawyer-related poetry anthology. Michael Blumenthal introduced me to his publisher, Jack Estes, at Pleasure Boat Studio, a small literary press in New York, who agreed to publish a lawyer-related poetry anthology (all of the poetry by lawyers). *Lawyer Poets and That World We Call Law: An Anthology of Poems about the Practice of Law* was published by Pleasure Boat Studio in 2013. For a review of the anthology, *see*

Kate O'Neill, *Book Review: Lawyer Poets and That World We Call Law*, 11 Legal Communications & Rhetoric: JALWD 177 (2014).

Some fifty years prior to the publication of *Lawyer Poets and That World We Call Law*, Michie Company, a Charlottesville, Virginia, law book company, published a poetry anthology compiled by Percival E. Jackson, a lawyer and poet, under the title *Justice and the Law: An Anthology of American Legal Poetry and Verse* in 1960. The Percival Jackson anthology included the poetry of lawyers and other poets that focused, unfortunately, more on legal subject matter of the poems than on the quality of the poems.

When law reviews and law journals publish poetry they generally confine themselves to "legal verse." For a short historical survey of "legal verse," see J. Wesley Miller, "Legal Poetry," in *The Lawyer's Alcove*, at i–xii. On "legal verse," see generally Percival E. Jackson (ed.), *Justice and the Law: An Anthology of American Legal Poetry and Verse* (Michie Co., 1960); J. Greenbag Croke, *Poems of the Law* (William S. Hein, 1986) (S. Whitney, 1885); J. Greenbag Croke, *Lyrics of the Law: A Recital of Songs and Verses Pertinent to the Law and the Legal Profession* (William S. Hein, 1986) (S. Whitney & Co., 1884); and Irving Browne, *Law and Lawyers in Literature* (Wm. W. Gaunt & Sons, reprint, 1982) (Soule & Bugee, 1883). Legal verse seems to have found no significant place in the world of poetry generally, or in literary scholarship about poetry.

One does, of course, occasionally find a poem in a law journal. In earlier times, poetry was commonly found in journals like the *American Bar Association Journal* and *Case and Comment*, and in still older journals like *The Green Bag* (1889–1914). But, today, a poem in a law journal stands out like an exotic weed seeking cover in a hostile habitat, its only protective coloration being the fact that it is "legal verse." The solitary poems we find in law journals are so overshadowed by the heft and hardiness of the species that surround them, they are easy to overlook. We suspect that most law readers ignore these fugitive law-themed poems in professional journals in the way so many ignore poetry wherever it appears. In the poetry anthology issue of the *Legal Studies Forum*, we created a place where poems are no longer required to compete for attention.

For indexes to the poetry published in the *ABA Journal* and *Case and Comment*, see appended indexes to the reprint edition of Ina Russelle Warren (ed.), *The Lawyer's Alcove: Poems by the Lawyer, For the Lawyer and About the Lawyer* (William S. Hein & Co. 1990) (reprint edition) (Doubleday, Page, 1900). For an index to the *Green Bag* poetry, see "Green Bag Poetry Index," in *The Lawyer's Alcove*. The old *Green Bag* has been thoughtfully, brilliantly reinvented, beginning publication in 1997 as a "second series" of the old *Green Bag*. The new *Green Bag 2d* holds itself out to be an "entertaining journal of law" and we have found it so, much as law, literature, and politics provided entertainment in Chautauqua days. Unfortunately, *Green Bag 2d* features little poetry.

In the years I published the poetry of lawyers in the *Legal Studies Forum*, most of the poems were of the kind, the nature, that any poet might produce.

For the poetry that appeared in *LSF*, I never subscribed to the idea that because *LSF* was a legal journal, the subject matter of the poetry should be legal in nature. Most lawyer poets make no effort to call attention, in their poems, to their association with the legal profession.

Legal verse has always had a rather nasty reputation among poets, and with the exception of Charles Reznikoff, and the fact that non–lawyer poets will from time to time address a matter of law, or justice, in their poetry, legal verse is a genre of poems that historically deserved its lowly status. And yet, when I reread the *LSF* poetry, I found a fair number of worthwhile poems that would historically be categorized as legal verse. Day in and day out, as a trickle of law-related poems came my way, I published the best of them. They were, I might note, never the lesser work of the poets, and were often quite readable; I was honored to publish these poems.

I had no idea that the poems that appeared in *LSF* would provide poems for an anthology of contemporary poetry that would focus on the work and the life of lawyers and their thinking about law. Then, I realized that lawyer poets write in the same compelling, poignant, powerful way about themselves and their work as they do about song birds, snowstorms, winter accidents, love affairs (some in winter and some in summer), everyday life, and cosmic speculation. I had never been a fan of legal verse until I realized that of the living lawyer poets I admired, some had written in their poetry about their lives as lawyers, sometimes about the law, in compelling ways. When David Kader and Michael Stanford published their anthology of law-related verse, *Poetry of the Law: From Chaucer to the Present* (University of Iowa Press, 2010), and included only the work of six contemporary lawyers (Lawrence Joseph, Brad Leithauser, Seth Abramson, Martín Espada, along with Edgar Lee Masters and Charles Reznikoff, and a Canadian lawyer poet, Roy Fuller) with most of the anthology devoted to poets who had no training in the law, I decided that it was time to revisit the idea of an anthology of poetry about lawyers and their work, their lives and their thinking about law, an anthology limited to poetry by lawyers. The result: an edited selection of lawyer subject poems collected from the poems published in the *Legal Studies Forum*, an anthology titled *Lawyer Poets and That World We Call Law: An Anthology of Poems about the Practice of Law* (Pleasure Boat Studio, 2013).

8   The contemporary poets whose work appeared in *Off the Record: An Anthology of Poetry by Lawyers* published by the *Legal Studies Forum* in 2004 include: Helen Bailey, Richard Bank, Peter Baroth, Mel Belin, Ace Boggess, Gary Botting, Sara Jane Boyers, David Bristol, Robert Bunzel, Daniel Caine, Joseph Caldwell, Esther Cameron, Karl Carter Jr., Christine Demimonde, Larry Joe Doherty, Marc Ellis, Martín Espada, Richard Falk, David Filer, Josey Foo, Michael Friedman (now deceased), Iris Gomez, Friedrick Haines, Nancy Henry, Gregory Hobbs (now deceased), Susan Holahan, Paul Homer (now deceased), Lawrence Joseph, Ilya Kaminsky, William Keener, Lillian Baker Kennedy, T. S. Kerrigan, Kenneth King, David Krieger, Laurie Kuribayashi, W. Adam Mandelbaum, Barry Marks, Greg McBride, Michael McPherson (now deceased), Jake

Miller, Sonia Alisa Montalbano, Tim Nolan, Jim Nye, Raymond Zachary Ortiz, Michael Parish, Charles Patterson, Simon Perchik (now deceased), John Perrault, Alice Persons, Frank Pommersheim, Jendi Reiter, George Reitnour, Steven Richman, Barbara Rollins, Steven Rood, Lawrence Russ, Ellen Sazzman, Gregory Shaffer, Beecher Smith, Gerry Spence, Mike Sutin (now deceased), Richard Taylor, Joseph Thackery (now deceased), Jesse Weiner, James Whitley, Warren Woessner.

The poetry anthology, *Off the Record*, represents the first effort of a United States legal journal to devote an entire issue to poetry. Law journals do, of course, publish poetry, but they do it sparingly, and when they publish a poem it is usually a poem about law or the practice of law. The poets whose work appears in the anthology write poetry not for their colleagues in the legal profession, but for readers of poetry, for fellow poets, and, of course, for themselves. Many of the lawyer poets included in the anthology have published widely and received recognition for their poetry.

V

reading the poetry of lawyers with students

LET ME SEE IF I CAN EXPLAIN what otherwise might seem like a rather odd proposition: I decide to teach a course on lawyer poets and their poetry. I was delighted to find students willing to sign up for Lawyers, Poets & Poetry when I first offered the course in 2006 (and further offerings of the course in 2012 and 2017). To my knowledge, no course on lawyers and poetry had previously been taught in an American law school.[1]

Students who found their way to Lawyers, Poets & Poetry arrived with a host of questions: What is this course? What will we do in the course? Will we really read poetry? (What poetry?) Will we be asked to write poetry? If I know nothing about poetry should I avoid taking the course? Do you need to be a literature major to take the course? Is the course in any way remotely related to becoming a lawyer? Or is this a spring-break-in-Cancun kind of course? Questions of this kind are expected; expectations are heightened when a student steps off the beaten-path to enroll in a course like Lawyers, Poets & Poetry. Given the unusual nature of the course, I want to tell students the story behind the course. What follows (with some inevitable repetition) is what I tried, in three versions of the course, to convey to students about what to expect and what might lie ahead:

■

In the Lawyers, Poets & Poetry course, you can expect to read poetry.[2] (I can assure you: You will not be asked to write poetry.) A regard for poetry may (or may not) have attracted you to the course; a disdain for poetry would certainly prevent most students giving any thought of signing up for the course.

■

A limited selection of the poetry we read in Lawyers, Poets & Poetry will focus on law and lawyers; most of the poems we read have nothing to do with law and, on first glance, appear to have no relevance to the fact that you have set out to become a lawyer. Lawyers, when they become poets, make little use of their poetry for observations about law and the world they inhabit as lawyers. Most lawyer poets have nothing to say in their poetry about law or the practice of law. We can assume that lawyers, with notable exceptions, use poetry to escape the legal world they inhabit and focus their poetry and themselves on the world beyond law.[3]

■

What possible rationale can you have for introducing law students to poetry? The simple (and yes, insufficient) answer: The poetry was written by lawyers. Having chanced upon the poetry of lawyers, I want to see if we can find a place for this poetry in your education as a lawyer.

■

What I have in mind for students in Lawyers, Poets & Poetry is the kind of freedom lawyers create for themselves in becoming poets: freedom that comes from inhabiting a world that exists less in the form of "necessities" and more in the way of "gifts." In Lawyers, Poets & Poetry, this means finding a way to see the poems presented to you less as *assigned texts* more as *gifts* from lawyers who have made the effort to attain the skills of a poet. This does not mean that every poem you read will find a welcome home; what it means entails being receptive to poems that invite rereading, poems you puzzle over, poems that locate a fissure in your present understanding of your self and the world you now inhabit.

■

With so many people reading less, it is not surprising that most of us don't read poetry. Yet, poetry flourishes . . . hundreds of chapbooks and collections of poetry are published every year. The world of poets and poetry seems to be flourishing. But this does not explain my invitation to read poetry in law school.

■

We don't think of law students as being the kind of student who would have even the remotest interest in poetry. Your presence in Lawyers, Poets & Poetry calls into question the stereotype that accompanies this kind of thinking about law students.

■

If you have a head full of conventional images of *lawyer* and *poet*—and who does not?—I admit that I labor with these stereotypes—then this idea of a lawyer poet is something of an oddity—a curiosity—a source of puzzlement. On first impression, we tend to think that lawyers and poets exist in different universes.

■

Lawyers have been poets from the days colonists first arrived in America. You may regard this fact—curious, odd, salient, revelatory—or just an artifact to be filed away in your mental in-box.

■

Lawyers continue to present themselves to the world as poets; lawyers routinely publish their poetry alongside the work of other poets. Hundreds of practicing lawyers in the United States are published poets. In my library, I have chapbooks and collections of poetry written and published by 363 contemporary lawyer poets. Who would have known we have so many lawyers who are poets? Curious, you might think: being a lawyer and a poet. Curious enough to read their poetry?

■

Some twenty years ago, intrigued by the presence of poets in the legal profession, I set out to identify every lawyer poet in America.[4] No one, so far as I could determine, had ever attempted anything of this kind. We have long known that celebrated twentieth-century poets—Wallace Stevens, Archibald MacLeish, Edgar Lee Masters—were lawyers. My research, posted on a website (Strangers to Us All: Lawyers and Poetry) on Labor Day, September 3, 2001, suggests that lawyers have been more extensively involved in poetry and literary culture than anyone has previously documented.

■

I make no claims about what connects lawyers to poetry, what might bring a lawyer to become a poet, or how a lawyer might put poetry to use in his understanding of law or his day-to-day lawyer work.[5] Reading the poetry of lawyers, it becomes clear that most lawyer poets don't find a place in their poetry for poems about the law or their work as lawyers. What this suggests, I suspect, is that when lawyers write poetry they see themselves inhabiting a world beyond law. When I discovered that lawyers were poets and set out to read their poetry, I wasn't in search of poetry about law and lawyering. Knowing a lawyer wrote the poetry provided an impetus for me to read it; I did not look to the poetry of lawyers to learn anything about the practice of law or to marvel at the novelty of law presented in verse form. What I found most intriguing—something to puzzle over—was this odd juxtaposition: *poet | lawyer*.

■

Lawyers, Poets & Poetry is a course in which you will be introduced to poetry. The idea is that you can learn something from poetry and can find the poetry you need to learn something of value.

■

Another proposition: It is never too late to start reading poetry. To read poetry, you don't need a guide or a teacher to help you figure out that what you are reading has meaning for you. My advice for students who find that law school is a boot-camp of the mind: Read a collection of poetry every semester you are in law school.[6] Read poetry along with your daily diet of judicial opinions. Reading poetry might end up making more sense than you might think. If you have not been a reader of poetry—most of us have not—then your willingness to do something different, get off the narrow path prescribed for you in law school, is notable. You may find, surprisingly, that reading poetry can be an enjoyable part of the day. Reading poetry may help you become a better reader—a better student—more attentive—more alive.

■

A colleague, a practicing lawyer and a published poet, bolstered my spirits when he claimed I was "brave" to offer the Lawyers, Poets & Poetry course. I am reticent to think I might be brave; what I most want to think is that I can avoid being foolish in what I have set out to do. I know some students tell me they are excited that such a course is being offered in law school. And yes, they too may be a bit apprehensive. I will try to ease their apprehension (and my own) with the working belief that every student in the course can take pleasure in reading the poetry of lawyers (if the selection of poetry presented is judiciously selected). We have interesting (difficult) work ahead of us. Difficult, I think, in the sense that we will inevitably puzzle over what we are to do with the poetry we read.

■

It was my friend Carl Reisman, an Urbana, Illinois, lawyer, author of collections of poems, *Kettle* (Hot Lead Press, 2005) and *Home Geography* (Stone City Press, 2008), who sought to bolster my spirits by suggesting I was "brave to jump into these waters"—teaching a course on poetry in law school. Reisman applauded the "room for serendipity" I designed into the course and went on to offer his own thoughts on "different ways" and "approaches" we might take in the course. Reisman framed his comments on the course with a question: "What, if anything, does this poetry you invite students to read offer as a sort of trail marker?" He posed this question with the understanding that students "might be uncertain about how they might be lawyers and maintain (or even develop) their humanity. Does reading the poems in the course aid in finding one's way?" Reisman refers to a characterization of a poet from 1900: "[A poet is] endowed with the gift and power of imaginative invention and creation attended by corresponding eloquence of expression, commonly but not necessarily in metrical form" (*The Century Dictionary and Cyclopedia*). Reisman suggests this well-aged description of a poet "conflicts with our ideas of who a lawyer is and what a lawyer does." The question for the law student is this: "What is the conflict and how can it be resolved?" Reisman goes on to ask: "Whatever possessed lawyers to write poetry? Poetry is a pursuit with few readers, many writers—it's not unusual for a literary magazine to have five hundred submissions of poetry for every poem accepted—no money, no fame. It's difficult to think of an art form that is less marketable. What would make someone who is in a profession like law that is so mercenary do something so unprofitable, something that might be injurious to the lawyer's reputation as a fearless litigator?" Reisman suggests a way to think about this puzzling question—why would a lawyer write poetry? "Law school is a ritual of initiation. In law school there is magic and mystification, the death of an old identity and the birth of the new professional self. For a lawyer poet, writing poetry may be a vestige of the old identity, something that didn't burn away, or it may be the core of the new identity." The email presenting these ideas was signed: "Just some musings. Courage, warrior professor, Carl." My note to Carl: Encouragement when it was most needed.

■

To follow up on Carl Reisman's thoughtful commentary, consider that legal education is commonly viewed in a critical light for its over-determined focus on *legal training* and its lack of focus on *education*. In Lawyers, Poets & Poetry the focus is on *education*.

■

What accompanies the traditional law school curriculum and culture is an *implicit curriculum*. Simply put, the *implicit curriculum* is that formative part of a student's education where legal training leaves off, where explicit instruction in law school runs out of steam. My colleague and friend Joseph Tomain, former dean at the University of Cincinnati Law School, observes that "students are left to feel their own way through the unlit halls of professional socialization."[7] Let me make a lofty claim for the poetry prescribed in Lawyers, Poets & Poetry: *Poetry is a way to install lighting in the unlit halls of professional socialization.*

■

A legal education is all about sharpening the mind by narrowing the mind. Poetry is all about sharpening the mind by opening the mind.

■

You may have teachers in law school who demand that you not only read assigned judicial opinions but that you read them closely. (And you may, faced with this demand for "close reading," be curious about how this kind of reading is done.) Teachers may suggest you read cases critically. (And, again, you ask, how is this "critical reading" done.) You may be asked to not only read cases but reflect on what you have read. (The implication seems to be that "reflective reading" is different from other kinds of reading.) We might note that close reading, critical reading, and reflective reading are literary-focused approaches to reading that are as applicable in the study of law as they are in the study of literature. Poetry invites close, critical, reflective reading; poetry makes you more attentive to how you read.

※

Reading poetry, you may find: You are more attentive to language—that you seek out language that is compelling—observe how the jeweled precise use of language stripped bare and stretched tautly can be a thing of beauty—surprise yourself with delight in the presence of configurations of language that demand exploration in unexplored reaches of the world law would have you know.

※

Exactly what you may have had in mind when you signed up for Lawyers, Poets & Poetry—what you might be looking for—what you expect to find in the course—intrigues me.

※

How you regard poetry, how you regard what you are invited to read, depends in large part on what you bring with you to the course. The *baggage* you bring with you to the course cannot be ignored. The course may have its own *character* but what you make of this character, depends on the way you read the poetry.

■

I did not require a pledge of allegiance to poetry as a prerequisite for enrolling in the course. I have the hope—consider it an arrogance of belief if you will—that I have found poetry that will appeal to you. I am reminded of this statement by Edgar A. Poe about our deep-lying poetic sentiment: "The principles of the poetic sentiment lie deep within the immortal nature of man, and have little necessary reference to the worldly circumstances which surround him."[8] I don't find Poe to be suggesting that every reader will come around to a declaration of a love of poetry; what Poe seems to be saying is that there is something about poetry, about what poetry does and how it goes about doing what it does that resonates with sentiments that lie "deep within" us. If you learn, as a student in Lawyers, Poets & Poetry that you don't have any hint of poetic sentiment anywhere in your makeup, you may conclude that Poe was wrong about "poetic sentiment" belonging to our "nature." If you come to this realization about your own lack of poetic sentiment, I trust you will want to see what insight you might gain about the underlying cause of your condition. The Poe statement is all the more interesting in his finding that the existence of "poetic sentiment" in men and women has little relationship to their "worldly circumstance." What we want to do in Lawyers, Poets & Poetry is to see how our "worldly circumstance" might look differently when we read poetry.

■

Clarence Darrow, who at one time practiced with two lawyer poets, Edgar Lee Masters and Ernest McGaffey, is reputed to have said: "Inside every lawyer you'll find a wreck of a lawyer poet." I want to think you have an inner poet. Whatever you think of poets, this inner poet is not something you want to arrogantly silence. William Carlos Williams, a physician and acclaimed modern-day poet, told us this about poetry: "[M]en die miserably every day for lack of what is found there."[9] Who would think that a student of law has less need to be aware of their inner poet than anyone else?

■

I may have ended up reading poetry relatively late in life, but I now hold a firm conviction: *Any reader*, any law student who is a reader, can find poetry of use. What I bring to the course is simply this: *I am a reader*. I think of myself as a good reader. Even so, some of you will undoubtedly be better at reading poetry than I am.

■

Ezra Pound, in an essay titled "How to Read," observes that "Literary instruction in our 'institutions of learning' was, at the beginning of this century, cumbrous and inefficient" and he ventured to suggest "it still is."[10] I willing admit I received little in the way of "literary instruction" from institutions of learning. My failure to receive academic literary instruction might be seen as a prelude to disaster in any hope of success in teaching a course like Lawyers, Poets & Poetry. To counter this dire prediction, I ask you to engage in contrarian thinking: In having escaped university "literary instruction," I might end up being a friendlier guide and companion in Lawyers, Poets & Poetry than a teacher who has formal training in poetry. The danger of formal schooling: The teacher becomes pedantic. My *Webster's Seventh New Collegiate Dictionary* offers this definition of pedantic: "narrowly, stodgily, and often ostentatiously learned"; in short, "unimaginative" and "dull." I want to think that offering the Lawyers, Poets & Poetry course and your presence in the course, are, in wildly different ways, acts of imagination. We will stay on the lookout for anything that takes our reading of poetry in the direction of dull, stodgy, unimaginative.

■

I can tell you that my late blooming interest in poetry took me by surprise. Why an educated man should be surprised to find poetry intriguing, compelling, puzzling, mystifying is more than a little odd. An educated person would know that poets and poetry, viewed by some with disdain, are held in high regarded for a reason. That poetry has a place in one's reading life should not be a surprise—a mystery.

■

Being a reader all my life—life within the reach of memory—I have never taken anything akin to a vacation from reading. My time in law school was no exception. How exactly, I managed to spend a lifetime reading and came to poetry so late remains a mystery I have yet to resolve. Part of that mystery might be explained by the fact that I have never, reading what I do, followed a plan, or sought advice. In reading, I have sailed in whatever direction the winds would take me. Whether I should lay this situation to a lack of discipline or being overly endowed with curiosity is an open question. The effects of being undisciplined, being my own teacher, are tendencies (foibles?) I have learned to live with.

■

Wendell Berry, an acclaimed essayist and novelist, is an accomplished poet—a Kentucky farmer. Wendell Berry, more than anyone else I might try to name, has helped me understand, through his poetry, novels, and essays, how I carried Kentucky with me over the years. I became a reader of Wendell Berry's poetry, not because I have an affinity for poetry, but because I think it worthwhile to read anything Wendell Berry might write.[11] I know that it means something, something more than I can easily assess or give an account, that I was raised on a Kentucky farm. Some part of my thinking of what that might mean, I learned from Wendell Berry.

■

Poetry, for most of us, lies in a far distant universe. Some of us have no familiarity with poetry. Others, exposed to poetry, find that exposure did not leave a lasting imprint. We assume, based on personal experience, that we can live without poetry. We pay little attention to those who step forward to argue the vital significance of poetry. We assume, that by some fate, an exquisite few of us became poetry aficionados who speak in high praise of poetry that most of us find a way to ignore.

■

In Lawyers, Poets & Poetry, I make an essential claim: Poetry can be made a part of your education as a lawyer. This is a claim you will want to use your reading of poetry to consider. What is this poetry, of what use can it be? The question, most basically, is this: Is there any poetry, of any kind, poetry someone might invite you to read—poetry you can read with pleasure, poetry that might be, in some way, instructive? In Lawyers, Poets & Poetry, I want to think you will find your way to an affirmative answer to this question.

■

What lies in poetry must be discovered. Your interest in poetry—an interest that will accompany you through the course—depends upon what you find in the poetry you are invited to read.

> You read a poem—nothing seems to happen
> (the world doesn't tilt on its axis)
> the poem lies inert on the page
> a text among text
>
> you read another poem—
> the still air moves
> a slight welcome breeze
> on a consummate summer day
>
> the poet reaches for something
> something remarkable
> something commonplace
> the poet creates new light

■

We *discover* poetry that matters to us. You don't need a teacher's instruction or a guidebook to poetry to make this discovery possible.[12] We *discover* poetry that matters to us in much the same way we find our way to music. I turn on the car radio. Without realizing what I am doing, I tune from station to station. I don't have

Sirius in the car, so there is no way of knowing what kind of music will be in the offering. With all the music available, I rarely hear anything I find appealing, nothing that sounds like music to me. It may be music to others; it doesn't work as music for me.

■

Imagine someone—a stranger—arrives in your neighborhood, goes from door to door, announcing that you and your neighbors would benefit from making a place for poetry in your reading. The stranger departs with this admonition—*read poetry*. You decide, much to your own surprise, to take the stranger's advice. You go to Barnes & Noble where you find shelves of poetry books: poetry by established poets like Robert Frost, Walt Whitman, Edgar Lee Masters, Emily Dickinson, T. S. Elliot, Wallace Stevens. You find collections of poetry by poets who have, against the odds, garnered an audience—Billy Collins, Mary Oliver, Robert Pinsky. Even this limited array of possibilities can leave you a little bewildered, if not overwhelmed. (Keep in mind that whatever we encounter that lies beyond our familiar world has the potential to overwhelm us.) Perusing the poetry books you find at Barnes & Noble, you may not find poetry you want to pursue. Finding poetry that captures your attention turns out to be more difficult than anticipated. You decide you might need some kind of guide. *Let someone knowledgeable about poetry make the selection of what it might be best to read.* A marginally informed clerk at Barnes & Noble might point you to an anthology of the kind used in introduction to poetry classes: *The Norton Anthology of Poetry* (6th ed., 2013), or perhaps, *The Oxford Book of American Poetry* (Oxford University Press, 2006). If a bookstore with shelves of poetry books is intimidating, the Norton and Oxford massive poetry anthologies may further test your patience and your fortitude. There is fine poetry to be found in these bloated anthologies, but a collection of our best poets and their most celebrated poems may not be the best way to find poetry.[13]

■

Can I find poetry that I can read for pleasure and for insight? Your first response may be something like this: "Well, there may be poetry out there that would get the job done, but who in the world would make the effort to seek it out. In my case, reading the poetry of lawyers and thinking about their lives has drawn me to poetry in a way I could never have imagined or foretold. My hope is that Lawyers, Poets & Poetry will prove to be a source of poetry you actually want to read—poetry that can be elusive to find.

■

So here is the question: Will this poetry I invite you to read in Lawyers, Poets & Poetry become poetry you find engaging and instructive? Poetry you will take delight in reading? Will there be poems that pull you down into your self, poems that pull you away from what feels familiar, poems that awaken an interest in the studied ways that poets have found to express their reverence for language?[14] When I discovered lawyer poets, I found poetry I wanted to read. And what poems are you willing to read that become more than *assigned texts*? Consider: Poems you eagerly reread. Poems you find intriguing—compelling—insightful—informing—haunting—lyrical. Poems that speak to some part of your present life and the life you envision for yourself. Poems that speak to parts of you that are ignored or dismissed in your law-school confined life. Poems you carry with you.

■

In Lawyers, Poets & Poetry, you are invited to use your reading of poetry to create a personal anthology of poetry.[15] Imagine this anthology being composed and configured in a way that allows you to account for how you have made your way to poetry, how you have sought to make poetry a part of your education. Consider the kind of introduction you will need to tell the reader something about the poets you decided to include and something about the selection of poems that comprise the anthology. In this anthology work, you are being asked to put to use what you have learned from the poetry you have read in the course, in particular what you have learned about your self.

■

Faced with the task of creating an anthology, introducing the poems (and the poets) in the anthology, you may be concerned about being asked to do something you have no previous experience doing. In law school, you expect to be pushed beyond your familiar world, pushed to explore unknown terrain and experience the chaos that lies beyond your known explored world.[16] Testing your adaptability in traversing unknown terrain is something of a hallmark of the law school experience. Think of reading poetry like this: You are on a foray into the unknown.

■

I suspect that you know more about anthologies than you might realize.[17] Doesn't a law school casebook with its collection of judicial opinions look something like an anthology? You might think of the Bible as an anthology—a collection and amalgamation of stories, parables, historical vignettes, presented alongside advice, admonishments, and prophecies.[18]

■

In composing an anthology, you might give some thought to what purpose you have found in reading poetry—the poetry of lawyers. I have a sense, once you start reading poetry, you will find a purpose in the reading from the particular poems that stand out for you.[19]

■

We read poetry to deepen and expand the conversation we have with ourselves (and others), to find ways—often new ways—to talk intelligibly about our lives and the world we inhabit. Talk incessantly about our lives as we do, it is the poet who creates artifacts of this struggle, artifacts we use to see our own world with greater clarity. We honor the poet for saying what seems so inescapably hard to say, for being, in a poem and in life, a seeker of intelligent use of language.

■

Wallace Stevens, one of our most celebrated lawyer poets, says that poetry is "a response to the daily necessity of getting the world right."[20] Lawyers, like poets, are in the practice of "getting the world right." Lawyers and poets have a good deal to say to each other about what they have set out to do in the world. "This is why we need poetry in our lives: to remind us that life could be different."[21] Robert Bringhurst observes that "lawyers, doctors, teachers and engineers, like bakers, potters and carpenters, all have to be poets in their own way. When they are not, things are apt to go awry. And they do go awry, because professions become institutions, and institutions close their doors and windows, leaving poetry outside."[22]

■

Our most basic questions about poetry, its value, its use, have always been with us. Here is one statement of the question from one hundred fifty years ago:

> What is poetry good for? what does it prove?—are questions very like to be propounded by some of our busiest men, whatever may be their profession, whenever they are invited to judge for themselves by reading, at least, a brief review of what is called a poem,—being of those who, when they are pestered with invitations to run away from their business for awhile, when the woods are flowering and the cheerful waters are singing for joy, excuse themselves by saying they can't see the use of it; or they don't believe it will pay. When business is good, they cannot spare the time; and when it is bad, they can't spare the money; and so they go on year after year, like a squirrel in his cage, traveling the same dreary round, without ever trying to escape, though the door be sometimes left open, until they get to be men of one idea—in other words, no better than monomaniacs; for what were our many faculties given us, if only a few are to be exercised? Were they not all intended for use? And shall a man . . . be satisfied with growing old over his desk, and counting his gains every night before he goes to sleep . . . ? Shall he,

having ears, hear not, by stopping them to music, when the bewildering harmonies of well-managed concert, or the rhythm of a stately, noble poem, are filling the air about him?—eyes, and see not, when the glories of architecture and sculpture and painting are all about his way? What were such men made for? only to neglect or abuse their gifts? to concentrate all their powers upon the gathering of riches? or upon the gathering of riches? or upon president-making? or, indeed, upon any one pursuit or occupation, forgetful of every other?[23]

■

Do we "need" poetry today? It would seem most of us experience no pressing need for poetry. (Something of a similar sort might be said about the man on the street who, in his daily life, doesn't think well of lawyers and has no apparent need for what a lawyer has to offer.) And so we find, those of us left untouched by the hand of the Muse, that we assume we have no observable need for poetry. *But is it actually possible—to live untouched by what we find poetic?* We may well have need of poetry that goes unrecognized and unacknowledged, a need we do not know how to articulate (or to identify).

■

What makes poetry, and thus the work and life of the poet of special interest to us, special enough to study and puzzle over? Do we misunderstand our poets (and, for that matter, misunderstand lawyers, psychiatrists, scientists) because we know so little of their practices and about what they try to do with language and the sensibilities they express in their devotion to particular uses of language? Perhaps, the poet and the lawyer see the world in a nuanced way that demands the world be addressed with the best possible language, language that calls attention to itself, language that sets itself apart by form and appearance, by the sound of it when spoken.

Both poetry and law are acquired tastes. Are we not surprised by our lawyer poets who have acquired a taste for both law and poetry?

I begin and end the Lawyers, Poets & Poetry course thinking: *I have found poetry you will find worth reading. We take up this poetry, initially, because it was composed by fellow lawyers. We find, perhaps surprisingly, that poetry can be a far more easily acquired taste than we would have predicted. More surprising, we find in reading poetry that this reading has a place in forming the mind that has a taste for law.* I'm anxious to see how this thinking holds up under close scrutiny. Curious, you ask: What is this poetry? How did you happen to find it? What makes you think this poetry you have discovered will be of interest to me in the life I have set out to live? The answer to these questions is a story, a story I was pleased to tell in Lawyers, Poets & Poetry.

Chapter V
Endnotes

1. Days before submitting the manuscript of *Discovering Our Lawyer Poets* for production, I happened upon a *Harvard Law Today* newsletter dated April 19, 2022, that presented a statement from Jessica Fjeld, a lecturer on law at Harvard, in the form of a headline: "I'd love it if poetry was required reading for law school." Jessica Fjeld is a published poet; her collection of poetry titled *Redwork* was published by BOATT Press in 2018. Fjeld holds an MFA in poetry from the University of Massachusetts and a JD from Columbia Law School. We learn from the *Harvard Law Today* news account that Fjeld sponsored a spring 2022 reading group, "Thinking Like Yourself: Poetry, Law, and Social Justice." The reading group purportedly focused on lawyer poets. Exactly which lawyer poets we are not told.

2. In the 2017 version of the course, the final offering before my retirement in 2019, virtually all of the poetry presented in the course was drawn from poetry published in the *Legal Studies Forum*, with the primary source being *A Legal Studies Forum Poetry Anthology*, 41 Legal Stud. F. 1–657 (2017).

3. For students who determine the value of any poetry they might read based on its "relevance" to lawyers and the practice of law, the Lawyers, Poets & Poetry course could have been based on the poems found in James R. Elkins (ed.), *Lawyer Poets and That World We Call Law: An Anthology of Poems*

    about the Practice of Law (Pleasure Boat Studio, 2013).

4   For the result of my effort to identify every lawyer poet in America, *see* Appendix: A Chronological Index of Lawyer Poets.

5   For a ground-level look at what it might mean to be a lawyer and a poet, *see* Tim Nolan, "Lawyer Poets and the Practice of Law," in James R. Elkins (ed.), *Lawyer Poets and That World We Call Law: An Anthology of Poems about the Practice of Law* 15–18 (Pleasure Boat Studio, 2013). For an expanded version of the Nolan essay, *see* Tim Nolan, *Poetry and the Practice of Law*, 46 S. D. L. Rev. 677 (2001). Tim Nolan's published poetry includes: *The Sound of It* (2008), *And Then* (2012), *The Field* (2016), all by New Rivers Press, and *Lines: Poems* (Nodin Press, 2022).

6   This suggestion—Each Year of Law School—Read a Collection of Poems—first appeared in James R. Elkins, *The Law School Journey: A Calendar of Readings* 201–205 (Carolina Academic Press, 2020).

7   Joseph Tomain, *Epilogue*, 38 J. Legal Educ. 629, 631 (1988).

8   Edgar A. Poe, *Griswold's American Poetry*, 2 (5) Boston Miscellany of Literature & Fashion 218 (1842).

9   The quoted phrase is from William Carlos Williams's long poem "Asphodel, That Greeny Flower." In context: "It is difficult / to get the news from poems / yet men die miserably every day / for lack / of what is found there." The poem appears in William Carlos Williams, *Journey to Love* 56 (Random House, 1955).

10 "How To Read," *in* T. S. Eliot (ed.), *Literary Essays of Ezra Pound* 15–40, at 15 (New Directions Book, 1968).

11 A collection of poems I continue to read over the years is Wendell Berry's *Farming: A Hand Book* (Harcourt Brace Jovanovich, 1970). During the course of my work with lawyer poets, another collection of Wendell Berry's farmer poems appeared: Wendell Berry, *The Mad Farmer Poems* (Counterpoint, 2014).

12 "Some students bring their own ardency—their own 'soul-hunger'—to the literature they read, some discover a dormant ardency awakened by their professor, but almost all students require the guidance and the knowledge a teacher offers to fill the hunger that they bring, to not only delight in literature but also to find in it the possibility of utter transformation—the possibility, each time, of conversion." Abram Van Engen, *Reclaiming Claims: What English Students Want From English Profs*, 5 (1) Pedagogy: Critical Approaches to Teaching Literature, Language, Composition & Culture 5, 15 (2005).

13 It is most definitely the case that you may chance upon friendlier anthologies than the *Norton* and *Oxford* introduction to great poetry anthologies. Garrison Keillor has edited several anthologies that might be a better place to look for poetry that will work for you. A place to start: Garrison Keillor (ed.), *Good Poems* (Viking, 2002).

14 On this rather peculiar notion of making the familiar strange, consider the situation in which the student of law finds herself: She begins the study of law enveloped in a familiar world. Legal educators take

it as their task to help the student recast and reconfigure this familiar world into a new universe, taking the familiar and giving it new names that require categories of thought that embrace a different way of valuing that gives rise to a different scheme of meaning. We immerse students of the law in what can feel not just different, but strange, and we whisper to them: "This isn't so bad, is it? It may be new and strange to you now, but you will get the hang of it. This is the way everyone becomes a lawyer. You will become one of us soon enough. The days of strangeness will pass." Given this steady—if arrhythmic—translation of familiar to strange, there is the counter: Soon enough the strange will begin to feel familiar. Doesn't this particular description of what takes place in law school begin to look, in some way, like the law student invited to read poetry?

Anthony G. Amsterdam and Jerome Bruner, in *Minding the Law*, remind us: "There are many ways of making the familiar strange . . . . Juxtaposing the past and the present is surely one way—the historian's honored way of quickening consciousness. But it is no mythic whim that Clio, the Muse of History, has four sisters who are muses to poets of diverse sorts. For poets, like historians, toil relentlessly to estrange the familiar, though they do it differently. Their tropes and metaphors, conceits and images and evocations cut across our daily, dulled perceptions of the world and lure us, even yank us, out of the banality of routine." Anthony G. Amsterdam & Jerome Bruner, *Minding the Law* 4 (Harvard University Press, 2000). Edward Hirsh reminds us that, "[t]he poem refreshes language, it estranges and makes it new." Edward Hirsch, *How to Read a Poem: And*

Fall in Love with Poetry 12 (Harcourt Brace & Co., 1999).

Wallace Stevens, a lawyer poet well known in legal and literary circles, observed: "I and you, and all of us live in a monotony which would be all right except for the horrid disturbances that come chiefly from within ourselves." Wallace Stevens's letter to Henry Church, dated May 18, 1943, in Holly Stevens (ed.), *Letters of Wallace Stevens* 448–449, at 449 (University of California Press, 1996) (1966). There are any number of poets, lawyer poets among them, who would amend Stevens to include recognition that the disturbances that prompt poetry are not only from "within ourselves," but from without, as we are disturbed by what we see in the world outside us as we are from what we find within us.

15 For another teacher's invitation to students to compose—and introduce—an anthology based on their reading of poetry, *see* Laura L. Aull, *Students Creating Canons: Rethinking What (and Who) Constitutes the Canon*, 12 Pedagogy: Critical Approaches to Teaching Literature, Language, Composition & Culture 497, 508, 509 (2012).

16 On how we experience existential reality in terms of our familiar and unfamiliar worlds, worlds explored and unexplored, known and unknown world, *see* Jordan B. Peterson, *Maps of Meaning: The Architecture of Belief* (Routledge, 1999); *12 Rules for Life: An Antidote to Chaos* (Random House Canada, 2018); *Beyond Order: 12 More Rules for Life* (Portfolio/Penguin, 2021).

17 "[W]e are all . . . every day of our lives, and to a greater degree than we habitually acknowledge,

anthologists and anthology-makers . . . . Teachers and students are . . . constantly forced to select and prioritise, to remove, and set in various kinds of rearrangement, tiny fragments and moments from the vast body of material of which they originally formed a part." David Hopkins, *On Anthologies*, 37 (3) Cambridge Quart. 285, 286 (2008).

18 This view of the Bible—reading it like an anthology—is presented with no intent to engage in theological debate about how this particular view of the Bible may take the reader in one direction or another.

19 The poet T. R. Hummer, commenting on the purpose of poetry, observes that: "I approach the task of describing that ineffable 'something' [we associate with poetry] with the same apprehension Randall Jarrell felt on being asked what he did for a living by a stranger in the next airplane seat. It is difficult to explain to others just what we are up to as poets; one is tempted simply to point to the poems and leave it at that. But that isn't fair to people of good will who find the profession of poetry puzzling."

Hummer goes on to say, "For the culture, I am convinced, poetry functions . . . for the engaged individual reader . . . [like] an electrification, a reminder that there *are* real mysteries left." T. R. Hummer, *Available Surfaces: Essays on Poetics* 1 (University of Michigan Press, 2012).

20 "'Adagia,' From the Notebooks," in *Wallace Stevens: Collected Poetry & Prose* 900–914, at 913 (Library of America, 1997). (Selection and notes by Frank Kermode & Joan Richardson.)

21 Peter Horn, "Poetry in Our Lives Today," Internet-Zeitschrift für Kulturwissenschaften, 1997, (https://www.inst.at/trans/0Nr/phorn.htm).

22 Robert Bringhurst, *Everywhere Being is Dancing: Twenty Pieces of Thinking* 74 (Gaspereau Press, 2007).

23 1 (6) Putnam's Magazine: Original Papers on Literature, Science, Art & National Interests 718 (1868). (No author or title of the commentary.)

Epilogue

twenty-two propositions

■

I . . . subscribe to the view—not original with me—that the world is constructed in such a way as to be as interesting as possible.

. . . .

When you think intensely and beautifully, something happens. That something is called poetry.

—Robert Bringhurst, "Poetry and Thinking," in
The Tree of Meaning: Thirteen Talks 139–158,
at 158, 143 (Gaspereau Press, 2006)

■

poets are everywhere
no need to starve your self
of what they offer
drown yourself in poetry
then—swim ashore
as if nothing happened

-1-
poetry illuminates a world
inside the known world we inhabit

-2-
poetry is one way we reconfigure
the world we now call our own

-3-
poetry refuses to leave
the lazy dog undisturbed

-4-
poetry makes a demand on you
on your belief in language
poets encourage us
to double down on our bet on this belief

-5-
poetry reads best in the early morning
before the day settles in
necessity calls your name

-6-
you will, no doubt, chance upon poems
—quiet poems   —noisy poems
—flat poems   —exuberant poems
the world is scattered with poems
find poems that mean something to you

-7-
put aside poems that don't appeal to you
draw near every poem you find appealing

-8-
step around noisy poems
find another patron

-9-
poems are dime a dozen
don't panic if you read all morning
come up empty-handed

-10-
find poems to read
again & again

-11-
create your own anthology

-12-
poetry is an act of discovery
make a place for something new in your life

-13-
be thankful
discover poems that inform you about the life
you are living—the life you are not living

-14-
let poems take you
into quiet recesses
of your unlived life

-15-
a poem from the bow of a practiced archer
travels the distance—hits its target

-16-
when you encounter
something strange in a poem
call it mystery

-17-
the poet goes places
where there is meager light
to see the world again—poem by poem

-18-
poets steer us around the mundane
poets take us to that very place
from which they help us escape

-19-
what lies ahead, you ask—
fate will tell
poetry lightens the load

-20-
praise for poetry is common
you too can sing this song

-21-
no need to starve your self
of what poets offer

-22-
drown yourself in poetry
then—swim ashore
as if nothing happened

    A phantasy of how it all happened: I am on a jaunt through life, editing a journal, taking on writing projects I can never expect to complete, teaching courses that invite students to think about what it means to be a lawyer . . . I fall through an unseen crevice into a small, dimly lit cavern library. The library houses a collection of several thousand books of poetry—astoundingly—all of the poetry has been written by lawyers. Reading, in a random manner, it becomes obvious that much of the poetry is out of fashion, discordant with our modern sensibilities. On one shelf of the library I find the poetry of contemporary lawyers who found a way to express their life beyond the law.

Appendix

a chronological index of lawyer poets (c. 1600-1950)

MY WORK WITH LAWYER POETS began with my introduction to John William Corrington's work in 2001. Lowell Komie and Marlyn Robinson were early supporters of my effort to undertake the historical literary excavation that resulted in this first catalogue of lawyer poets. Some of the lawyer poets included in the index are well-known literary figures, others are obscure figures, now lost in the debris of history.

Thomas Morton (c. 1579–1647)

Nicasius de Sille (1610–1674)
John Saffin (1626–1710)
Francis Daniel Pastorius (1651–1720)
Samuel Sewall (1652–1730)
Ebenezer Cooke (1667–1732)
Roger Wolcott (1679–1767)
Stephen Tilden (1687–1770)

Thomas Dale (1700–1750)
John Mercer (1705–1768)

Benjamin Pratt (1710–1763)
Thomas Rowley (1711–1796)

Peter Oliver (1713–1791)
Benjamin Waller (1716–1786)

William Livingston (1723–1790)
George Wythe (1726–1806)

John Gardiner (1731–1793)
John Dickinson (1732–1808)
Francis Hopkinson (1737–1791)
Asahel Clark (1737–1822)

Alexander Martin (1740–1807)
Nathaniel Niles (1741–1828)
George Chalmers (1742–1825)
Samuel Field (1743–1800)
John Lowell (1743–1802)

Thomas Burke (c. 1747–1783)
Jonathan Mitchell Sewall (1748–1808)
Hugh Henry Brackenridge (1748–1816)

John Trumbull (1750–1831)
St. George Tucker (1752–1828)
Joel Barlow (1754–1812)
William Bradford (1755–1795)
Stephen Jacob (1755–1816)
Henry Mellen (1757–1809)
Henry Brockholst Livingston (1757–1823)
John Leeds Bozman (1757–1823)
Thomas Dawes (1757–1825)
Royall Tyler (1757–1826)
Archibald Stuart (1757–1832)
William Moore Smith (1759–1821)
William Rawle (1759–1836)

Humphrey Marshall (1760–1841)
Samuel Dexter (1761–1816)
Joseph Bartlett (1762–1827)
St. John Honeywood (1763–1798)
John Allen (1763–1812)
Chauncey Lee (1763–1842)
Return Jonathan Meigs (1764–1825)
William Sampson (1764–1836)
Prentiss Mellen (1764–1840)
Theodore Dwight (1764–1846)
Manoah Bodman (1765–1850)
Daniel Stebbins (1766–1856)
John Quincy Adams (1767–1848)
Joseph Dennie (1768–1812)
Josias Lyndon Arnold (1768–1796)

William Littell (1768–1824)
John Coalter (1769–1838)

David Everett (1770–1813)
Anthony Bleecker (1770–1827)
Joseph Hopkinson (1770–1842)
Charles Brockden Brown (1771–1810)
Thomas Green Fessenden (1771–1837)
John Lathrop Jr. (1772–1820)
Benjamin Whitwell (1772–1825)
William Wirt (1772–1834)
Philip Carrigan (1772–1842)
Robert Treat Paine Jr. (1773–1811)
Isaac Story (1774–1803)
William Merchant Richardson (1774–1838)
Allan B. Magruder (1775–1822)
William Munford (1775–1825)
James Elliott (1775–1839)
Thomas Kennedy (1776–1832)
Charles Pinckney Sumner (1776–1839)
John Alsop (1776–1841)
Andrew Coffinberry (1778–1856)
Charles Hammond (1779–1840)
Francis Scott Key (1779–1843)
Joseph Story (1779–1845)

Samuel Haines (1780–1825)
Samuel Bellamy Beach (1780–1866)
Horace Binney (1780–1875)
John Blake White (1781–1859)
John Wilson Campbell (1782–1833)
Daniel Webster (1782–1852)
Andrew Wallace (1782–1856)
Charles Jared Ingersoll (1782–1862)

William Czar Bradley
(1782–1867)
William Bartlett Sewall
(1782–1869)
John E. Hall (1783–1829)
Jesse Lynch Holman
(1783–1842)
George Watterston (1783–1854)
William Freeman (1783–1879)
Guy Humphrey McMaster
(1783–1879)
Nathaniel Beverley Tucker
(1784–1851)
William Maxwell (1784–1857)
John Lewis (1784–1858)
James William Gazlay
(1784–1874)
John Pitman (1785–1864)
John Pierpont (1785–1866)
Gulian C. Verplanck (1786–1870)
William Ebenezer Richmond
(1786–1873)
Nathaniel Wright (1787–1824)
William Crafts (1787–1826)
Tobias Rudulph III (1787–1828)
Nathan Lansford Foster
(1787–1860)
William Rudolph Smith
(1787–1868)
John Robertson (1787–1873)
Richard Henry Dana Sr.
(1787–1879)
Enoch Lincoln (1788–1829)
Nathaniel Hazeltine Carter
(1788–1830)
Peter Wagener Grayson
(1788–1838)
William J. Grayson (1788–1863)
Charles Stewart Daveis
(1788–1865)
Richard Henry Wilde
(1789–1847)

William Plumer Jr. (1789–1854)
Moses Brooks (1789–1869)
Nathaniel Appleton Haven
(1790–1826)
Alexander H. Everett
(1790–1847)
Job Durfee (1790–1847)
Francis Calley Gray (1790–1856)
Theodor Erasmus Hilgard
(1790–1873)
Marshall Carter (1791–1820)
Frederick Knight (1791–1849)
James Athearn Jones
(1791–1854)
Jeremiah Fellowes (1791–1865)
William Orlando Butler
(1791–1880)
Nathaniel Deering (1791–1881)
George Mifflin Dallas
(1792–1864)
Townsend Haines (1792–1865)
Josiah Pierce (1792–1866)
John Barton Derby (1792–1867)
John Henry Hopkins
(1792–1868)
Seba Smith (1792–1868)
Amos Andrew Parker
(1792–1893)
Edwin Clifford Holland
(1793–1824)
Micajah Autry (1793–1836)
John Cadwalader McCall
(1793–1846)
James Hall (1793–1868)
John Neal (1793–1876)
Nathaniel Peabody Rogers
(1794–1846)
Cyrus Wadsworth Hart
(1794–1854)
William Cullen Bryant
(1794–1878)

Henry Denison (1795–1819)
Daniel Bryan (1795–1866)
John Pendleton Kennedy
 (1795–1870)
David Paul Brown (1795–1872)
John Gardiner Calkins
 Brainard (1796–1828)
Thomas Hedges Genin
 (1796–1868)
George Kent (1796–1884)
Charles Edwards (1797–1868)
Charles Carter Lee (1798–1871)
Ellis Lewis (1798–1871)
Bellamy Storer (1798–1875)
Charles West Thomson
 (1798–1879)
Robert C. Sands (1799–1832)
Grenville Mellen (1799–1841)
Josiah Andrews (1799–1847)
Oliver William Bourn Peabody
 (1799–1848)
Richard Penn Smith (1799–1854)

Benjamin Brown French
 (1800–1870)
Alfred Johnson Cotton
 (1800–1875)
Caleb Cushing (1800–1879)
William Henry Sparks
 (1800–1882)
Harvey Rice (1800–1891)
John Everett (1801–1826)
George W. Cutter (1801–1865)
Nathaniel Gookin Upham
 (1801–1869)
Elijah Huntington Kimball
 (1801–1893)
Edward Coote Pinkney
 (1802–1828)
Asa Moore Bolles (1802–1832)
William Bernard Conway
 (c. 1802–1839)

Albert Gorton Greene
 (1802–1868)
George Denison Prentice
 (1802–1870)
Fortunatus Cosby Jr. (1802–1871)
Armistead Burt (1802–1883)
William Betts (1802–1884)
Harvey D. Little (1803–1833)
William Post Hawes
 (1803–1843)
Rufus Dawes (1803–1859)
Jonathan Dorr Bradley
 (1803–1862)
Richard Hampton Vose
 (1803–1864)
George Lunt (1803–1885)
Frederic Mellen (1804–1834)
Otway Curry (1804–1855)
Caleb Stark (1804–1864)
Fredrick Pinkney (1804–1873)
Robert Rantoul Jr. (1805–1852)
Nathaniel Ingersoll Bowditch
 (1805–1861)
Joseph Hulbert Nichols
 (1805–1862)
Michael Doheny (1805–1863)
William George Crosby
 (1805–1881)
James Barr Walker (1805–1887)
Charles Fenno Hoffman
 (1806–1844)
William Gilmore Simms
 (1806–1870)
Michael Johnston Kenan
 (1806–1875)
Robert Boodey Caverly
 (1806–1887)
George Western Thompson
 (1806–1888)
Moody Currier (1806–1898)
Isaac McLellan Jr. (1806–1899)
Micah P. Flint (1807–1830)

Hugh Peters (1807–1831)
Jonathan Lawrence
 (1807–1833)
Robert M. Charlton (1807–1854)
Edward Sanford (1807–1876)
John Patch (1807–1887)
Enoch Lloyd Cowart
 (1807–1889)
Philip Battell (1807–1897)
Theodore Sedgwick Fay
 (1807–1898)
Henry Reed (1808–1854)
Benjamin Faneuil Porter
 (1808–1868)
Lewis Foulk Thomas
 (1808–1868)
Salmon P. Chase (1808–1873)
William Wragg Smith
 (1808–1875)
John Brown Dillon (1808–1879)
James D. Davidson (1808–1882)
Charles S. Bryant (1808–1885)
Stephen Selwyn Harding
 (1808–1891)
Benjamin Bussey Thatcher
 (1809–1840)
John Williamson Lowe
 (1809–1861)
Park Benjamin (1809–1864)
Sidney George Fisher
 (1809–1871)
Edmund Burke (1809–1882)
Salathiel C. Coffinberry
 (1809–1889)
James McCauley (c. 1809–1890)
Albert Pike (1809–1891)
George W. Snow (1809–1900)

James H. Perkins (1810–1849)
Jesse Walker (1810–1850)
Robert Taylor Conrad
 (1810–1858)

Alfred W. Arrington
 (1810–1867)
John Hickman (1810–1875)
Robert Josselyn (1810–1884)
Henry Weld Fuller Jr.
 (1810–1889)
François Dominique
 Rouquette (1810–1890)
Joseph Addison Wing
 (1810–1894)
Caleb Earl Wright (1810–1899)
Charles James Fox (1811–1846)
Alexander K. McClung
 (1811–1855)
George W. Johnson (1811–1862)
Frederick W. Thomas
 (1811–1866)
Henri Rémy (1811–1867)
Sandford Cull Cox (1811–1877)
Alfred Billings Street
 (1811–1881)
Horace Peters Biddle
 (1811–1900)
John Osborne Sargent
 (1811–1891)
Charles D. Drake (1811–1892)
John Garaghty (1811–1895)
Henry Bedinger (1812–1858)
William Jewett Pabodie
 (1812–1870)
Oscar Lovell Shafter
 (1812–1873)
Peter Hamilton Myers
 (1812–1878)
T. Wharton Collens (1812–1879)
Charles H. Holmes (1812–1886)
Edward Henry Thomas
 (1812–1888)
Thomas Coffin Amory
 (1812–1889)
Aaron Barlow Olmstead
 (1812–1889)

John Rudolph Sutermeister (1813–1836)
Joseph Lyons (1813–1837)
John Turner Sargent Sullivan (1813–1848)
Henry Beck Hirst (1813–1874)
Israel Washburn Jr. (1813–1883)
George Vandenhoff (1813–1885)
Adrien Emmanuel Rouquette (1813–1887)
William Dana Emerson (1813–1891)
Daniel Ricketson (1813–1898)
Luther Rawson Marsh (1813–1902)
Charles Colcock Hay (1814–1856)
Henry W. Ellsworth (1814–1864)
George W. Pearce (1814–1864)
Alexander Beaufort Meek (1814–1865)
James Dixon (1814–1873)
William Howe Cuyler Hosmer (1814–1877)
James C. Bower (1814–1887)
Edward Payson (1814–1890)
William Erigena Robinson (1814–1892)
Daniel F. Miller (1814–1895)
Joel Prentice Bishop (1814–1901)
Nathaniel L. Sawyer (1815–1845)
Charles A. Jones (1815–1851)
Stoddard B. Colby (1815–1867)
James Topham Brady (1815–1869)
John S. Reid (1815–1879)
Levi Bishop (1815–1881)
Richard Henry Dana Jr. (1815–1882)
Edmund Flagg (1815–1890)
Robert L. Johnson (1815–1890)
George Washington Dunn (1815–1891)
John Babson Lane Soule (1815–1891)
William Russell Smith (1815–1896)
Philip Pendleton Cooke (1816–1850)
David Barker (1816–1874)
Robert Tyler (1816–1877)
Robert William Wright (1816–1885)
John Godfrey Saxe (1816–1887)
Severn Teackle Wallis (1816–1894)
Edmund Stephen Holbrook (1816–1897)
Philippe Régis Denis de Keredern de Trobriand (1816–1897)
Charles Patrick Daly (1816–1899)
Albert Gallatin Riddle (1816–1902)
George Alexander Wheelock (1816–1906)
Elihu Spencer Miller (1817–1878)
Gideon Hiram Hollister (1817–1881)
Cornelius Mathews (1817–1889)
Miles Tobey Granger (1817–1895)
William Paterson (1817–1899)
George W. Lamb (1818–1853)
William Turner Haskell (1818–1859)
Benjamin Apthorp Gould Fuller (1818–1865)
Joseph Clarkson Passmore (1818–1866)

John Albion Andrew
(1818–1867)
Nathan Armsby Woodward
(1818–1900)
Joseph A. Nunes (1818–1904)
John Thomas Lindsay
(1818–1906)
James Thomas Aldrich
(1819–1875)
William Ross Wallace
(1819–1881)
Richard Don Wilson
(1819–1883)
Spencer Wallace Cone
(1819–1888)
Steuben Jenkins (1819–1890)
James Russell Lowell
(1819–1891)
L. A. Norton (1819–1891)
Donn Piatt (1819–1891)
William Wetmore Story
(1819–1895)
Thomas Dunn English
(1819–1902)
William Trimble McClintick
(1819–1903)
Martin Russell Thayer
(1819–1906)
George Foster Talbot
(1819–1907)
William McClung Paxton
(1819–1916)

Edward Erasmus Sargeant
(1820–1858)
Theodore O'Hara (1820–1867)
Henry Howard Brownell
(1820–1872)
B. F. Washington (1820–1872)
Norman L. Brainerd
(1820–1877)
Leonard Case (1820–1880)

George Vandenhoff
(1820–1885)
Jonathan W. Gordon
(1820–1887)
Joseph W. Winans (1820–1887)
Columbus Drew (1820–1891)
William Gibbs McAdoo
(1820–1894)
Henry Rootes Jackson
(1820–1898)
William Wilkinson Green
(1820–1899)
Clarence Augustus Walworth
(1820–1900)
George Douglas Brewerton
(1820–1901)
Albert Mathews (1820–1903)
William Read Scurry
(1821–1864)
Charles Noble Emerson
(1821–1869)
Oliver Cromwell Gray
(1821–1871)
Charles Oscar Dugué
(1821–1872)
William Hubbard (1821–1872)
Frederick Goddard Tuckerman
(1821–1873)
William Furniss (1821-1882)
Edward Dean Rand (1821–1885)
James Bowen Everhart
(1821–1888)
Divie Bethune Duffield
(1821–1891)
Alvin Peterson Hovey
(1821–1891)
James Simmons (1821–1899)
Sylvester Genin (1022–1050)
John Henneberry Green
(1822–1861)
George Edward Rice
(1822–1861)

Maunsell Bradhurst Field (1822–1875)
William Henry Rhodes (1822–1876)
Eugene Batchelder (1822–1878)
John Q. A. Wood (c. 1822–1881)
George Lynn (1822–1886)
Thomas J. Evans (1822–1889)
Jonathan Jones Marvin (1822–1891)
Jacob Wardwell Browne (1822–1892)
James Webb Rogers (1822–1896)
John Wilford Overall (1822–1899)
Edward John Phelps (1822–1900)
William Cant Sturoc (1822–1903)
Henry Lee Fisher (1822–1909)
Charles Phelps Roberts (1822–1914)
Cornelius Cole (1822–1924)
Philo Henderson (1823–1852)
Lewis Dela (1823–1856)
Edward Pollock (1823–1858)
James Mathewes Legaré (1823–1859)
Thomas Reade Rootes Cobb (1823–1862)
Buehring H. Jones (1823–1872)
John Reuben Thompson (1823–1873)
David Atwood Wasson (1823–1887)
James Valentine Campbell (1823–1890)
John Randolph Tucker (1823–1897)
James Watson Gerard (1823–1900)
William H. Bushnell (1823–1901)
H. P. H. Bromwell (1823–1903)
Isaac Hoover Julian (1823–1910)
Richard Frederick Fuller (1824–1869)
George Henry Miles (1824–1871)
George Boyer Vashon (1824–1878)
Joseph Brownlee Brown (1824–1888)
William Addison Phillips (1824–1893)
Anthony Q. Keasbey (1824–1895)
John Evans (1824–1896)
John Augustine Wilstach (1824–1897)
Thomas McIntyre Cooley (1824–1898)
George Bennett (1824–1900)
Charles Godfrey Leland (1824–1903)
James F. Harney (1824–1904)
William Edward Gilmore (1824–1908)
John McDowell Leavitt (1824–1909)
Gideon Tabor Stewart (1824–1909)
Joseph Hartwell Barrett (1824–1910)
Henry Beebee Carrington (1824–1912)
Reuben Thomas Durrett (1824–1913)
Benjamin Tupper Cushing (1825–1850)
Robert Pleasants Hall (1825–1854)
William Whiteman Fosdick (1825–1862)

Nathan Ames (1825–1865)
Samuel Jenkins Hay
  (1825–1881)
Augustus Julian Requier
  (1825–1887)
Charles William Goddard
  (1825–1889)
William Allen Butler
  (1825–1902)
John D. Bail (1825–1903)
Fernando Cortez Searl
  (1825–1904)
John Gosse Freeze (1825–1913)
William Haines Lytle
  (1826–1863)
Thaddeus Oliver (1826–1864)
Joseph Addison Turner
  (1826–1868)
William Stark (1826–1873)
Edward Delafield Smith
  (1826–1878)
Charles Green Came
  (1826–1879)
Henry Schell Hagert
  (1826–1885)
William Clark Falkner
  (1826–1889)
John Lewis Cole (1826–1890)
Robert Carter Richardson
  (1826–1896)
Abraham Oakey Hall
  (1826–1898)
Gideon John Tucker
  (1826–1899)
Elijah Whitter Blaisdell
  (1826–1900)
Thomas Durfee (1826–1901)
Coates Kinney (1826–1904)
Francis Wayland (1826–1904)
James F. Simmons (1826–1905)
Augustus Aurelius Coleman
  (1826–1910)

Lucius Harwood Foote
  (1826–1913)
John Rollin Ridge (1827–1867)
William Belcher Glazier
  (1827–1870)
John Marchborn Cooley
  (1827–1878)
John Bodwell Wood
  (1827–1886)
Thomas Webb (1827–1894)
Charles Theodore Hart Palmer
  (1827–1897)
George Vaughn Strong
  (1827–1897)
Robert Hawley (1827–1905)
Logan E. Bleckley (1827–1907)
William Hoag Bristol
  (1828–1853)
Theodore Winthrop (1828–1861)
James Johnston Pettigrew
  (1828–1863)
Henry Timrod (1828–1867)
Augustin Louis Taveau
  (1828–1886)
George Parker Smoote
  (1828–1891)
Konrad Krez (1828–1897)
John Walker May (1828–1899)
James Chute Peabody
  (1828–1900)
James De Ruyter Blackwell Sr.
  (1828–1901)
Jacob Smith Barnhart
  (1828–1906)
Eben Wallace Kimball
  (1828–1923)
Norman Williams Bingham
  (1829–1862)
José Agustín Quintero
  (1829–1885)
James Barron Hope (1829–1887)
Albert Laighton (1829–1887)

George Edwin Bartol Jackson
(1829–1891)
William James Jones
(1829–1894)
Peleg Stone Perley (1829–1898)
Abel Beach (1829–1899)
Henry Thayer Niles (1829–1901)
Will Cumback (1829–1905)
William Pinkney Ewing
(1829–1907)
Dewitt Clinton Duncan
(1829–1909)
Josiah Phillips Quincy
(1829–1910)
Franklin Jay Parmenter
(1829–1912)
Rodney Keene Shaw
(1829–1913)
David Fletcher Hunton
(1829–1915)
James Monroe Ritchie
(1829–1918)

Charles Alanson Munger
(1830–1873)
S. Edwin Ireson (1830–1874)
Edward James O'Reilly
(1830–1880)
John Esten Cooke (1830–1886)
Paul Hamilton Hayne
(1830–1886)
Edward Willet (1830–1889)
Benjamin Homer Hall
(1830–1893)
William D. Morange (1830–1895)
William Penn Boudinot
(1830–1898)
Truman Harvey Purdy
(1830–1898)
Edward Fitch Underhill
(1830–1898)
Robert C. Fraim (1830–1903)

John E. Van Etten (1830–1904)
Francis Browning Owen
(1830–1905)
William Henry Koontz
(1830–1911)
Gay H. Naramore (1830–1914)
George Augustus Wilcox
(1830–1928)
Howard Hayne Caldwell
(1831–1858)
Hiram Ozias Wiley (1831–1873)
William Preston Johnston
(1831–1899)
Ignatius Donnelly (1831–1901)
Charles Carroll Bonney
(1831–1903)
Patrick Cudmore (1831–1916)
Jonathan E. Hoag (1831–1927)
John Archer Clarke (1832–1862)
Orsamus Charles Dake
(1832–1875)
Charles H. Collins (1832–1904)
William Dunham Snow
(1832–1910)
William Wallace Harney
(1832–1912)
C. Augustus Haviland
(1832–1918)
William Bartlett Sewall
(1833–1869)
David Harmmons Hill
(1833–1879)
John Wiltse Lee (1833–1880)
William Tilghman Haines
(1833–1884)
Richard S. Spofford
(1833–1888)
John James Ingalls (1833–1900)
Joseph Blythe Allston
(1833–1904)
John Wheeler Moore
(1833–1906)

George Norman Corson
(1833–1907)
Lucius Horatio Biglow
(1833–1909)
Melville Weston Fuller
(1833–1910)
Michael Moores Teager
(1833–1910)
Benjamin S. Parker (1833–1911)
Cyrus Elder (1833–1912)
Josiah Stoddard Johnston
(1833–1913)
Isaac Bassett Choate
(1833–1917)
George V. A. McCloskey
(1833–1933)
W. T. G. Weaver (1834–1877)
Hugh Farrar McDermott
(1834–1891)
Edward Sprague Rand, Jr.
(1834–1897)
Henry Thompson Stanton
(1834–1898)
Charlton T. Lewis (1834–1904)
William Vicars Lawrance
(1834–1905)
Henry Oakes Kent (1834–1909)
George Henry Walser
(1834–1910)
Samuel V. Morris (1834–1913)
Joel Moody (1834–1914)
Irving Browne (1835–1899)
Joseph T. Hoke (1835–1910)
Albert Barnitz (1835–1912)
Egbert Phelps (1835–1916)
Leonard Stockwell Clark
(1835–1919)
John Aylmer Dorgan
(1836–1867)
Gaylord Judd Clarke
(1836–1870)
Edwin Gray Lee (1836–1870)
Daniel Webster Peabody
(1836–1879)
John Edwards (1836–1888)
Edwin Ethelbert Kidd
(1836–1895)
Thomas B. Long (1836–1900)
Henry Clay MacKrell
(1836–1900)
Theophilus Hunter Hill
(1836–1901)
James Daniel Lynch (1836–1903)
James B. Martindale
(1836–1904)
Needham Bryan Cobb
(1836–1905)
Samuel Calvin Tait Dodd
(1836–1907)
Frank Manly Thorn (1836–1907)
Bryon M. Cutcheon
(1836–1908)
Charles Francis Donnelly
(1836–1909)
Daniel Bedinger Lucas
(1836–1909)
Joseph Warren Gardiner
(1836–1916)
William Winter (1836–1917)
Hanford Lennox Gordon
(1836–1920)
Nathaniel Wilson (1836–1922)
Edward H. Lathrop (1837–1864)
William Stewart Hawkins
(1837–1865)
Patrick Egan (1837–1869)
James Innes Randolph Jr.
(1837–1887)
David Graham Adee
(1837–1901)
Hiram Howard Browne
(1837–1901)
Charles Elliott Mitchell
(1837–1911)

Joaquin Miller (1837–1913)
Fabius Maximus Ray
(1837–1915)
Basil W. Duke (1837–1916)
Timothy Edward Howard
(1837–1916)
Horatio Collins King
(1837–1918)
William A. Taylor (1837–1922)
James Braxton Thompson
(1838–1862)
Julius Walker Wright
(1838–1878)
George Washington
Cruikshank (1838–1900)
Thomas James Trussler
(1838–1900)
Wilson DeWitt Wallace
(1838–1901)
Arnold Green (1838–1903)
John Milton Hay (1838–1905)
John Staples White (1838–1908)
Samuel Lowrie Robertson
(1838–1909)
John Davis Long (1838–1915)
James Buckley Black
(1838–1916)
Edward Robeson Taylor
(1838–1923)
James M. Dalzell (1838–1924)
Samuel Hawkins Marshall
Byers (1838–1933)
George Jameson (1839–1887)
James Franklin Fitts
(1839–1890)
John Patrick Brown
(1839–1896)
Samuel D. Davies (1839–1900)
Robert Falligant (1839–1902)
Robert Nash Ogden (1839–1905)
John S. Stephenson
(1839–1905)

James Amaziah Whitney
(1839–1907)
Samuel Phelps Leland
(1839–1910)
Charles Leonard de Waele
(1839–1914)
Kinahan Cornwallis (1839–1917)
Milton Seward Griswold
(1839–1921)
Clara Hosmer Hapgood Nash
(1839–1921)
William Jonathan Davis
(1839–1925)
Horace Everett Warner
(1839–1930)

Robert Kelley Weeks
(1840–1876)
Leon da Silva Solis–Cohen
(1840–1884)
Albert Sobieski Twitchell
(1840–1901)
Edwin E. Parker (1840–1903)
James W. Stillman (1840–1912)
Levi F. Bauder (1840–1913)
Jacob David Oberlender
(1840–1917)
Rossiter Worthington
Raymond (1840–1918)
George Cooper (1840–1927)
John T. Lecklider (1840–1929)
Manlius T. Flippin (1841–1899)
Edward C. James (1841–1901)
Thomas Benton Ford
(1841–1903)
Randolph Rogers (1841–1907)
David Marshall Johnson
(1841–1908)
Joseph O'Connor (1841–1908)
John Brayshaw Kaye
(1841–1909)
Eugene Fitch Ware (1841–1911)

Henry Anson Castle
  (1841–1916)
William Tucker Washburn
  (1841–1916)
George Winslow Pierce
  (1841–1917)
Henry Melvil Doak (1841–1928)
Lewis Walter Keplinger
  (1841–1928)
Benjamin H. Fernald
  (1841–1929)
Thomas Elisha Hogg
  (1842–1880)
Sidney Lanier (1842–1881)
Daniel R. Lyddy (1842–1887)
Tim Needham (1842–1904)
Manly Tello (1842–1905)
John Akers Allen (1842–1908)
James B. Richmond
  (1842–1910)
Scott Rathburn Sherwood
  (1842–1910)
Philip Lindsley (1842–1911)
John Alexander Joyce
  (1842–1915)
Edward Lowell Anderson
  (1842–1916)
Crammond Kennedy
  (1842–1918)
William Henry Harrison
  Polhamus (1842–1919)
Charles Monroe Dickinson
  (1842–1924)
Clarence Augustus Buskirk
  (1842–1926)
John Preston Campbell
  (1842–)
Nelson B. Berryman
  (1843–1887)
Solon Noan Sapp (1843–1892)
Charles Louis Holstein
  (1843–1901)
Franklin Hubbell Mackey
  (1843–1904)
William Mathew Marine
  (1843–1904)
William Hubbell Fisher
  (1843–1909)
John H. Flagg (1843–1911)
W. C. Griffith (1843–1913)
David Morgan Jones
  (1843–1915)
William Temple Bell (1843–1916)
Samuel Whitaker Pennypacker
  (1843–1916)
Mary Hall (1843–1927)
Clark B. Cochrane (1843–1933)
Peter Jehu Malone (1844–1873)
James Sager Norton
  (1844–1896)
James Hooker Hamersley
  (1844–1901)
Maurice Thompson
  (1844–1901)
Frank Cowan (1844–1905)
Wallace Bruce (1844–1914)
Lucius Perry Hills (1844–1914)
James Hilary Mulligan
  (1844–1915)
Benjamin Franklin Waite
  (1844–1941)
John Edwards Leonard
  (1845–1878)
Charles Edward Pratt
  (1845–1898)
Samuel Leonidas Simpson
  (1845–1900)
Will Hubbard Kernan
  (1845–1905)
Henry James Coggeshall
  (1845–1907)
Charles H. A. Esling (1845–1907)
George Herbert Sass
  (1845–1908)

James W. Gibson (1845–1909)
Stillman Foster Kneeland
  (1845–1926)
William Wallace Scott
  (1845–1929)
Charles Gershom Fall
  (1845–1932)
Joseph S. Auerbach
  (1845–1944)
Richard Henry Savage
  (1846–1903)
George Edmund Otis
  (1846–1906)
Melville Madison Bigelow
  (1846–1921)
Frank McGloin (1846–1921)
Asahel Chapin (1846–1922)
M. V. Gannon (1846–1926)
Henry Lamm (1846–1926)
Maurice McKenna (1846–1927)
Orla Samuel Casad (1846–1928)
William Benjamin Munson
  (1846–1930)
Charles W. Bliss (1846–1931)
Howard Singleton Taylor
  (1846–1932)
John Scollay (1847–1890)
Joseph Peeples Hart
  (1847–1900)
Wesley Philemon Carroll
  (1847–1903)
William Henry Bliss (1847–1909)
Edwin James Foster
  (1847–1920)
Henry A. Beers (1847–1926)
Fay Hempstead (1847–1934)
George Montgomery Davie
  (1848–1900)
Joshua Soule Smith
  (1848–1904)
George Woodward Warder
  (1848–1907)
Garrett Barcalow Stevens
  (1848–1911)
William Caswell Jones
  (1848–1915)
Alonzo A. Rowley (1848–1916)
Will Henry Thompson
  (1848–1918)
John Vance Cheney
  (1848–1922)
Frank M. Vancil (1848–1923)
William Dudley Foulke
  (1848–1935)
James Niall McKane
  (1849–1878)
Henry Clay Fairman
  (1849–1896)
Charles Henry Noyes
  (1849–1898)
John R. Musick (1849–1901)
George Augustus Baker
  (1849–1906)
Charles E. Hoag (1849–1913)
Edward Payson Payson
  (1849–1914)
Andrew Augustus Gunby
  (1849–1917)
William H. Babcock
  (1849–1922)
Herbert Milton Sylvester
  (1849–1923)
William Gibbs Peckham
  (1849–1924)
Horatio Nelson Atkinson
  (1849–1933)
Harmon Seeley Babcock
  (1849–1937)
William Thomas Keller
  (1849–1939)

Francis Barnard Clark Jr.
  (1850–1896)
Orie Bower (1850–1901)

Richard Devereux Doyle
(1850–1909)
Isaac Rieman Baxley
(1850–1920)
Robert Franklin Walker
(1850–1930)
Mirabeau L. Towns (1850–1932)
William Alpha Paxson
(1850–1933)
Edwin M. P. Brister (1850–1910)
George King Camp (1851–1899)
C. C. Dail (1851–1902)
Daniel Henry Holmes Jr.
(1851–1908)
John Franklin Simmons
(1851–1908)
Charles Franklin Garberson
(1851–1921)
Frederick Fanning Ayer
(1851–1924)
James Manford Kerr (1851–1929)
John Emory Troutman
(1851–1931)
Charles William Buck
(1851–1932)
John Ruggles Strong
(1851–1941)
Graham Claytor (1852–1903)
Edward Rodolph Johnes
(1852–1903)
William E. S. Fales (1852–1906)
George Herbert Stockbridge
(1852–1916)
Paschal Heston Coggins
(1852–1917)
Herbert Van Allen Ferguson
(1852–1917)
Thomas James Macmurray
(1852–1918)
Louis Foulk Curtis (1852–1928)
(James) Brander Matthews
(1852–1929)

Nelson Williams (1852–1934)
Lyman Walter Seelye
(1852–1939)
Robert Grant (1852–1940)
George Grant (1852–1942)
Charles Erskine Scott Wood
(1852–1944)
Irwin Russell (1853–1879)
Bennett Thompson Bellman
(1853–1904)
Frank Conover (1853–1912)
William Eugene Houswerth
(1853–1919)
Thomas Nelson Page
(1853–1922)
Charles Eldridge Armin
(1853–1926)
Richard Thomas Walker Duke
Jr. (1853–1926)
Charles Luther Coyner
(1853–1928)
Henry Wayland Hill (1853–1929)
Daniel Joseph Donahoe
(1853–1930)
Chauncey Clinton Jencks
(1853–1932)
Charles Henry Phelps
(1853–1933)
Lyon Gardiner Tyler
(1853–1935)
Homer Greene (1853–1940)
George Frederick Cameron
(1854–1885)
William DeLancey Ellwanger
(1854–1913)
Walter Glasco Charlton
(1854–1917)
Daniel Peixotto Hays
(1854–1923)
Sam Kimble (1854–1924)
Charles Leonard Moore
(1854–1925)

Roswell Derby Jr. (1854–1927)
Ephraim Richard Eastman
   (1854–1931)
Alfred Ellison (1854–1934)
Charles Edmund DeLand
   (1854–1935)
Telford Groesbeck (1854–1936)
Bolton Hall (1854–1938)
Franklin D. Hale (1854–1940)
Samuel Craig Cowart
   (1854–1943)
Wilbur Richburgh Turner
   (1854–1946)
Belton O'Neall Townsend
   (1855–1891)
Columbus Moïse (1855–1895)
Robert Charles O'Hara
   Benjamin (1855–1900)
Albert Winston Gaines
   (1855–1916)
Wilbur Larremore (1855–1918)
John F. C. Waldo (1855–1923)
William Michie Coldwell
   (1855–1927)
Armistead Churchill Gordon
   (1855–1931)
Willis Boyd Allen (1855–1938)
Harry Stillwell Edwards
   (1855–1938)
Robert Morton Hughes
   (1855–1940)
Frank Willing Leach
   (1855–1943)
Ernest Howard Crosby
   (1856–1907)
William Walton Hoskins
   (1856–1910)
William Prescott Foster
   (1856–1915)
Thomas E. Watson (1856–1922)
Herbert Wolcott Bowen
   (1856–1927)
Charles Wells Russell
   (1856–1927)
Harry J. Chapman (1856–1930)
James Monroe Gibson
   (1856–1930)
Morris Gray (1856–1931)
Ethan Allen Hurst (1856–1931)
John E. Richards (1856–1932)
Philip Alexander Bruce
   (1856–1933)
William B. Gourley (1856–1935)
William W. Pfrimmer
   (1856–1935)
Edward Sanford Martin
   (1856–1939)
Jonah Leroy ("Doane")
   Robinson (1856–1946)
John F. Gontrum (1857–1909)
Charles J. O'Malley (1857–1910)
Tudor Jenks (1857–1922)
Gershom Mott Williams
   (1857–1923)
Will T. (William Thomas) Hale
   (1857–1926)
John Warren Gordon
   (1857–1931)
Samuel Alfred Beadle
   (1857–1932)
Lucius Matlack Fall (1857–1946)
A. H. Byrum (1857–   )
Will A. Davis (1857–   )
Traverse Eugene Stout
   (1858–1894)
William Bard McVickar
   (1858–1901)
John Paul Bocock (1858–1903)
Lee Light Grumbine
   (1858–1904)
Moses Irwin Stewart
   (1858–1905)
Henry Willard Austin
   (1858–1912)

Samuel Duffield Osborne
(1858–1917)
Fleming Tuckerman
(1858–1923)
Sidney Perley (1858–1928)
John Malcolm Harlow
(1858–1930)
Beecher Wesley Waltermire
(1858–1932)
Yates Snowden (1858–1933)
John Williams Barnes
(1858–1934)
Hiram Otis Bliss (1858–1935)
Luther Morton Keys
(1858–1935)
Williston Fish (1858–1939)
Rosewell Page (1858–1939)
John W. Beaumont (1858–1941)
Lettie Lavilla Burlingame
(1859–1890)
George Pellew (1859–1892)
Thomas Emmet Dewey
(1859–1906)
Thomas Walsh (1859–1913)
James Willis Gleed (1859–1926)
Samuel H. Smith (1859–1930)
A. McG. Beede (1859–1934)
Frank Boyd (1859–1937)
Edward Owings Towne
(1859–1938)
Robert H. Kane (1859–1939)
Edwin Henry Hackley
(1859–1940)
Charles H. Pearson (1859–1941)
Charles Hial Darling (1859–1944)
Edward E. Wright (1859–1944)
Henry Polk Lowenstein
(1859–1946)
Edward Franklin Taber
(1859–1950)
Wilmer W. MacElree
(1859–1960)

Walter A. McCausland
(1859–   )
James Lindsay Gordon
(1860–1904)
Alexander Clement Blount Jr.
(1860–1923)
Lester Shepard Parker
(1860–1925)
Douglas Dobbins (1860–1927)
James McNeill Johnson
(1860–1930)
John Elton Wayland (1860–1932)
J. Jerome Welty (1860–1934)
Hal Milford Perkins (1860–1937)
Constantine Peter Arnold
(1860–1943)
George B. Rose (1860–1943)
Frederick W. Fowler
(1860–1954)
Richard Nixon (1860–   )
Edwin Smith (1860–   )
Jackson Boyd (1861–1920)
Luther A. Lawhon (1861–1922)
Leon Fremont Moss (1861–1923)
Clarence Ladd Davis
(1861–1927)
John Luther Long (1861–1927)
Daniel Chauncey Brewer
(1861–1932)
George M. Bilger (1861–1934)
Daniel Leavens Cady
(1861–1934)
George Small Schmidt
(1861–1935)
Aloysius C. Gahan (1861–1936)
Ernest McGaffey (1861–1941)
Amos K. Mehl (1861–1941)
Joseph Allen Minturn
(1861–1943)
Thomas Emmet Moore
(1861–1950)

Wendell Philips Stafford
(1861–1953)
Tom Moore (1861–)
Harry Seward Chester
(1862–1906)
Robert Cameron Rodgers
(1862–1912)
George Grant Witty
(1862–1921)
Charles Washington Coleman
(1862–1932)
John Jay Chapman (1862–1933)
Langdon Elwyn Mitchell
(1862–1935)
Arthur Miller Easter
(1862–1936)
James Melmouth Hickman
(1862–1938)
George Beswick Hynson
(1862–1938)
Lysius Gough (1862–1940)
Thomas Ewing (1862–1942)
Howard S. Abbott (1862–1944)
John Steven McGroarty
(1862–1944)
Julius Miller Richardson
(1862–1947)
Lillien Blanche Fearing
(1863–1901)
Charles J. Barrett (1863–1907)
Andrew G. Lehr (1863–1914)
Ernest Lacy (1863–1916)
Rollin John Britton (1863–1931)
Charles Forrest Moore
(1863–1932)
Aaron Sherman Watkins
(1863–1941)
Miles Menander Dawson
(1863–1942)
Stanhope Henry (1863–1942)
Harvey Edgar Hoover
(1863–1945)
Joseph E. Acker (1863–1947)
Duncan McRa (1863–)
Richard Calmit Adams
(1864–1921)
Robert Loveman (1864–1923)
Thomas Fontaine Turner
(1864–1929)
Eli Richard Shipp (1864–1932)
Edgar Howard Fourt
(1864–1934)
James Tillman Williams
(1864–1935)
Howell Stroud England
(1864–1938)
Charles Elliot Branine
(1864–1939)
Solomon Levy Long
(1864–1940)
Sherman H. Makepeace
(1864–1945)
William West Smithers
(1864–1947)
Freeman Edwin Miller
(1864–1951)
J. T. Cotton Noe (1864–1953)
Ward D. Munholland
(1865–1906)
Albert Ulysses Lesher
(1865–1912)
Norris Clarion Sprigg
(1865–1930)
William De F. Totten
(1865–1932)
Miles J. Cavanaugh
(1865–1935)
Benjamin Jesse Gunn
(1865–1939)
Leonard Doughty (1865–1940)
Porter Byron Coolidge
(1865–1943)
Waldemar M. Seton Sr.
(1865–1945)

Francis Rives Lassiter
(1866–1909)
Walter Malone (1866–1915)
Harry Elliott Negley
(1866–1920)
Anthony Jerome Griffin
(1866–1935)
William Wisner White
(1866–1935)
James W. Falconer (1866–1938)
John Russell Hayes
(1866–1945)
John George Jury (1866–1945)
Edward S. Kremp (1866–   )
Francis Brooks (1867–1889)
Lloyd McKim Garrison
(1867–1900)
George Graham Currie
(1867–1926)
Marvin Hill Dana (1867–1926)
Charlie Lincoln McGuire
(1867–1926)
James Francis Burke
(1867–1932)
Ernest Fenwick Johnstone
(1867–1938)
John Jacob Cornwell
(1867–1953)
Charles Clinton Walsh
(1867–1943)
Claude Weaver (1867–1954)
Lucian Lamar Knight
(1868–1933)
Sheldon E. Bottsford
(1868–1935)
Herman A. Heydt (1868–1941)
Samuel P. Ridings (1868–1942)
Christopher Ward (1868–1943)
William Collett Tichenor
(1868–1947)
Lindley Grant Long
(1868–1949)

Edgar Lee Masters (1868–1950)
W. F. Button (1868–   )
Robert L. Walden (1868–   )
Philip Verrill Mighels
(1869–1911)
Charles Southern Morehead
(1869–1919)
Brand Whitlock (1869–1934)
Edward J. White (1869–1935)
Nathan C. Horton (1869–1946)
Eusebio Chacon (1869–1948)
Clay W. Metsker (1869–1949)
Claybron W. Merriweather
(1869–1952)

Vere Goldthwaite (1870–1912)
Samuel Francis Batchelder
(1870–1927)
Edward Bertram Finck
(1870–1931)
John Myers O'Hara (1870–1944)
James Stanislaus Easby–Smith
(1870–1948)
Jacob Gedaliah Grossberg
(1870–1950)
Hugh Aiken Bayne (1870–1954)
William A. Smith (1870–1958)
James C. Thomas (1870–1964)
Maurice H. Thatcher
(1870–1973)
Bur Conley (1870–   )
Jean La Rue Burnett (1871–1907)
Levi Wilbur Pollard (1871–1910)
William Richard Hereford
(1871–1928)
Joseph William Humphries
(1871–1930)
Andrew L. Price (1871–1930)
Clyde Beecher Johnson
(1871–1936)
Henry Haywood Glassie
(1871–1938)

James Weldon Johnson
(1871–1938)
George Hamilton Ethridge
(1871–1957)
Leon Hühner (1871–1957)
George Fauvel Gouraud
(1872–1915)
Gustave Frederick Mertins
(1872–1926)
Leroy A. Foster (1872–1934)
Max Ehrmann (1872–1945)
Charles Hall Davis (1872–1954)
David Perris (1872–1959)
Samuel Wallace Johnson
(1872–1964)
Charles Tilford Greene
(1873–1923)
John Milburn Harding
(1873–1934)
William Michael Fogarty
(1873–1936)
Orra Eugene Monnette
(1873–1936)
Mary Ray King (1873–1949)
John Truman Edson
(1873–1950)
John Cupp Lowe (1873–1950)
Arthur Orison Dillon
(1873–1958)
Charles Edmund Haas
(1873–1960)
John Charles McNeill
(1874–1907)
Russell Hillard Loines
(1874–1922)
Arthur William Beer (1874–1941)
Ernest Carl Klette (1874–1950)
Robert Restalrig Logan
(1874–1956)
Adele Ida Storck (c. 1874–1960)
James Naumburg Rosenberg
(1874–1970)

Bartlett Brooks (1875–1918)
H. Gerald Chapin (1875–1920)
Clement Yore (1875–1936)
Landon Chapman (1875–1937)
Daniel Irving Gross (1875–1945)
Thomas Lomax Hunter
(1875–1948)
George Albert Montrose
(1875–1950)
Samuel Page (1875–1952)
Daniel Maurice Robins
(1875–1956)
Jesse F. Brumbaugh
(1875–1959)
Charles Mumford Bush
(1876–1936)
William Clifford Archer
(1876–1950)
William Franklin Jenkins
(1876–1961)
Ila Earle Fowler (1876–1963)
Spencer Heath (1876–1963)
Henry Harvey Fuson
(1876–1964)
Edwin Milton Abbott
(1877–1940)
Harry Tennyson Domer
(1877–1942)
Walter H. Bonn (1877–1950)
David Horton Elton (1877–1963)
Joseph M. Proskauer
(1877–1971)
Marshal Azariah Byrnside
(1878–1946)
Walter Anthony Ryan
(1878–1948)
Lemuel Augustus Smith III
(1878–1950)
Jesse Sill (1878–1951)
John D. W. Bodfish (1878–1956)
Robert Sparks Walker
(1878–1960)

Emily Eva Mullenger Sloan
(1878–1973)
Dwight Gaylord McCarty
(1878–1974)
Lee Wilson Dodd (1879–1933)
James Owen Tryon (1879–1952)
Wallace Stevens (1879–1955)
Lawrence W. Neff (1879–1970)
Allen T. Luscas, Sr. (1879–1973)
Melville Henry Cane
(1879–1980)
Herbert B. Robinson (1879–   )

Benjamin Robbins Curtis Low
(1880–1941)
Davis Ben Johnson (1880–1952)
Thomas Reed Powell
(1880–1955)
Vincent Dante Calenda
(1880–1957)
Fred W. Goshorn (1880–1966)
George D. Copeland
(1881–1943)
Stewart Everett Rowe
(1881–1944)
Clifford Warren Axtell
(1881–1957)
Abraham Felt (1881–1957)
Albert Asche (1881–1959)
Donald Randall Richberg
(1881–1960)
Jennings C. Wise (1881–1968)
Harry Randolph Blythe
(1882–1915)
M. E. (Maude Edwin) Dunaway
(1882–1934)
Austin E. Walsh (1882–1935)
Jack Greenhill (1882–1970)
Edgar Aaron Hahn (1882–1970)
Albert R. Bandini (1882–1973)
Charles Ames Brooks
(1883–1931)

Clyde Walton Hill (1883–1932)
Edward Gay Hill (1883–1937)
Henry Wilbur Humble
(1883–1941)
Arthur Davison Ficke
(1883–1945)
Cecil B. Ruskay (c. 1883–1955)
McCune Gill (1883–1965)
Elias Lieberman (1883–1969)
James Grafton Rogers
(1883–1971)
Swinburne Hale (1884–1937)
Owen Friend Watkins
(1884–1965)
Florence Ellinwood Allen
(1884–1966)
Allan Davis (1885–1929)
William Alexander Percy
(1885–1942)
Arthur H. Ortmeyer
(1885–1943)
Joseph Whitla Stinson
(1885–1954)
James Hart Willis (1885–1963)
John French Wilson (1886–1946)
Anne Marie Evans (1886–1964)
Emory Aaron Richardson
(1886–1965)
Maurice Everett Allen
(1886–1966)
Samuel Barrett Pettengill
(1886–1974)
Abby Crawford Milton
(1886–1990)
Earl Darlington Van Deman
(1887–1931)
Victor Stanley Starbuck
(1887–1935)
Edward Leslie Spaulding
(1887–1939)
Rollin Leonard Smith
(1887–1942)

Merton L. Harris (1887–1944)
Edward Charles Schulze (1887–1966)
Martin Croissant (1887–1976)
Flora Warren Seymour (1888–1948)
Clement Wood (1888–1950)
William Henry Huff (1888–1963)
Newman Levy (1888–1966)
Benjamin Whipple Palmer (1889–1964)
Clarence P. Milligan (1889–1972)
Florence Meigs Beebe (1889–1973)
Robert Hale (1889–1976)
Clarence Edward Benadum (1889–1978)
R. Hawley Truax (1889–1978)
Francis Lyman Windolph (1889–1978)
Walter F. Wright (1889–1990)

Mitchell Dawson (1890–1956)
John B. Gontrum (1890–1963)
Lester Mardis Ackman (1890–1970)
Roy C. Bates (1890–1974)
Kurt Bauchwitz (1890–1974)
Ernst Lothar (1890–1974)
Augustus Longstreet Heiskell (1890–1980)
Harlan C. Allen (1891–1966)
Percival Ephrates Jackson (1891–1970)
Jess Perlman (1891–1984)
Augustine Joseph Bowe (1892–1966)
Scott Wike Lucas (1892–1968)
Archibald MacLeish (1892–1982)

Leo Horan (1892–1985)
Karl N. Llewellyn (1893–1962)
Arthur Lloyd Douglas (1893–1975)
Frank G. Swain (1893–1975)
Klein Kinzer Haddaway (1893–1980)
Walery J. Fronczak (1893–1986)
Norton Keys (1893–   )
Mark Greentree Sabel (1894–1934)
Luther Patrick (1894–1957)
Leigh Hanes (1894–1967)
Murray C. Bernays (1894–1970)
Edwardine Crenshaw Couch (1894–1972)
Duke Cole Meredith (1894–1972)
Julien Capers Hyer (1894–1974)
Charles Reznikoff (1894–1976)
Chard Powers Smith (1894–1977)
Irl Morse (1894–   )
Elizabeth Cody Johnson (1895–1979)
James A. Quinby (1895–1989)
Ilo Orleans (1897–1962)
Samuel Blauner (1897–1966)
John Williams Andrews (1898–1975)
Murrell Edmunds (1898–1981)
Amos Spencer Deinard (1898–1985)
Locke Miller (1899–1944)
Clyde Francis Murphy (1899–1946)
John C. H. Wu (1899–1986)

William M. Barrett (1900–1973)
Thomas P. Holt (1900–1978)
Andrew Denny Rodgers III (1900–1981)

Francis T. P. Plimpton
(1900–1983)
William Plumer Fowler
(1900–1993)
Rufus Lisle (1900–1997)
Charles Laban Abernethy Jr.
(1901–1968)
Frank Kleinholz (1901–1987)
Eli Greifer (1902–1966)
Leonard Bronner Jr.
(1902–1968)
Rudolph N. Hill (1903–1980)
Worth Wade (1903–1986)
David Randolph Milsten
(1903–1996)
Milton Jacob Goell (1904–1971)
Richard L. Sloss (1904–1975)
Carlos Ashley (1904–1993)
Michael J. McMorrow
(1904–1995)
John B. Sanford (1904–2003)
Albert Sherman Christensen
(1905–1996)
Edward Dumbauld (1905–1997)
Emmett Shelton Sr.
(1905–2000)
L. D. Covitt (1905–2001)
James J. Metcalfe (1906–1960)
Harold Rosenberg (1906–1978)
James Stafford (1906–1990)
George B. Clothier (1906–1992)
William R. Perl (1906–1998)
Fred Rodell (1907–1980)
Anton–Herman Chroust
(1907–1982)
Paul Phellis Dull (1907–1990)
Lakenan C. Barnes (1907–1998)
William Reese Scott (1907–1996)
James B. Gitlitz (1907–2002)
James Allen Wood (1907–2003)
Hy Zaret (1907–2007)
Eli Edgar Fink (1908–1979)

John Travers Moore
(1908–1994)
Henry Stone (1908–1998)
Calvin Hardin (c. 1908–2000)
Alfred W. Israelstam
(1908–2005)
Robert Martin Wash
(1908–2005)
Luis Kutner (1909–1993)
Raymond McCarty (1909–1995)
Mabel Rebecca Dole Haden
(1909–2007)
Elmer R. Haile (1909–2008)

Irving Wilner (1910–1984)
Pauli Murray (1910–1985)
Robert Kratovil (1910–1989)
Hamilton Lokey (1910–1996)
Reuben Lozner (1910–1998)
Harry Torczyner (1910–1998)
John Alexander "Jac"
   Chambliss Jr. (1910–2010)
Lenhardt Edwin Bauer
(1911–1986)
Louise Blackmar Hart
(1911–1987)
Howard Oleck (1911–1995)
Bernard S. Schwartz
(1911–2005)
Brainerd Currie (1912–1965)
John Alan Appleman
(1912–1982)
Ralph L. Kinsey (1912–1982)
Robert Athol Huston
(1912–1988)
Robert H. Burns (1912–1997)
Sidney K. Schoenwald
(1912–2007)
Albert De Pietro (1913–1989)
Byron B. Gentry (1913–1992)
Samuel F. Andewelt
(1913–2002)

Joseph P. McDonough
(1913–2004)
Sidney G. Sparrow (1913–2005)
Paula Adams Tennant
(1913–2010)
John Nantell (1914–1995)
Robert F. Weingartner
(1914–2004)
Edwin M. Adams Jr.
(1914–2008)
Frederick Koenig (1915–1978)
Bruce Redd McConkie
(1915–1985)
Francis Coleman Rosenberger
(1915–1986)
Charles L. Black (1915–2001)
Frank E. Taplin (1915–2003)
Joseph C. Thackery (1915–2007)
Joseph L. Alioto (1916–1998)
Henry Wilkins Lewis
(1916–2004)
Kenneth F. C. Murray
(1916–2005)
Seymour N. Harris (1916–2009)
Janet Oline Hart Diebold
(1917–1987)
Janet Hart Sylvester
(1917–1987)
Lee Ellen (Leola) Ford
(1917–1997)
Paul Golis (1917–2003)
Bruce McMarion Wright
(1917–2005)
Eugene A. Diserio (1917–2008)
Samuel Washington Allen
(1917–2015)
Charles Spaulding Thomas II
(1918–1981)
Bruce M. Wright (1918–2005)
Harold Norris (1918–2013)
William Moses Kunstler
(1919–1995)

Elreta Melton Alexander
(1919–1998)
K. Leroy Irvis (1919–2006)

Corbin A. Waldron (1920–1978)
Thomas Moncure (1920–1990)
Stewart Lee Udall (1920–2010)
Leonard Weintraub
(1920–2018)
John D. Ryan (1920–2011)
Warren Barrios Wilson
(1921– 2012)
Simon Perchik (1921–2022)
Robert Chasen (1922–1979)
Eugene Brooks (1922–2001)
Edward Boone Miller
(1922–2006)
John Richard Auchter
(1922–2011)
Chesley Venable Morton
(1923–1989)
Gloria Catherine Oden
(1923–2012)
Scott Conley (1923–2015)
Daniel G. MacLeod (1924–1997)
Vincent L. St. Johns
(1924–2006)
Edwin M. Zimmerman
(1924–2012)
Harry A. Ackley (1924–2013)
Hayes G. Dabney (1925–2002)
Saul Touster (1925–2018)
Harold Barnett McSween
(1926–2002)
Peter Heintz (1927–1996)
H. Eugene Johnson
(1927–2007)
Charlotte Mary van Stoll
(1927–2009)
Harry Waitzman (1927–2016)
James W. Symington (1927–   )
Burton Raffel (1928–2015)

Fred Simmons (1928–2018)
Jay Frankston (1928–2022)
Wilson Reid Ogg (1928–2023)
Stephen B. Wiley (1929–2015)
Gerry Spence (1929–)

Lawrence Pauley (1930–2017)
William Allen Watson
 (1930–2017)
Hayward D. Reynolds
 (1930–2020)
Margaret Waddell Peters
 (1931–1995)
George L. Dyer Jr. (1931–2006)
Theodore a. Borrillo
 (1931–2019)
Edward Packard (1931–)
Edward Siegel (1931–)
John William Corrington
 (1932–1988)
Carmine Florentino
 (1932–2001)
John E. Davis II (1933–1984)
William Mosolino (1933–2001)
Seth E. Frank (1933–)
Warren Wolfson (1933–)
James Liddy (1934–2008)
Garic Kenneth "Nikki"
 Barranger (1934–2015)
David Berman (1934–2017)
Richard J. Kittrell (1934–2024)
Oscar "Zeta" Acosta
 (1935–1974)
Michael G. Sutin (1935–2019)
James E. Ehrenfeld
 (1936–2002)
Judith G. Behar (1936–2016)
Ronald Garth Talney
 (1936–2019)
Herb Berman (1936–)
Marcus A. J. Smith (1936–)
James A. Costello (1937–2022)

T. S. Kerrigan (1939–2018)
Tom Gannon (1938–2021)
Thomas Fischer (1938–)
J. Iqbal Geoffrey (1939–2021)

Jan David Tissot (1940–2008)
Donald J. Heffernan
 (1940–2013)
John Acuff (1940–2021)
Patsy Anne Bickerstaff
 (1940–2023)
William S. Cohen (1940–)
Susan Holahan (1940–)
Judy Scales-Trent (1940–)
Allen Afterman (1941–1992)
Esther Cameron (1941–2023)
Tom Jones (1941–)
Richard Taylor (1941–)
Judith W. Constans (1942–2000)
Thomas Victor Siporin
 (1942–2001)
Ebon Dooley (1942–2006)
Frederick E. Fischer (1942–2011)
Dan Caine (1942–2015)
Richard S. Bank (1942–)
Howard L. Bass (1942–)
Dan Burt (1942–)
David Filer (1942–)
Joel Lipman (1942–)
Clark B. Cochrane (1943–2005)
John Bayard DesCamp
 (1943–2006)
Paul R. Rice (1943–2012)
Jesse Mountjoy (1943–)
Frank Pommersheim (1943–)
John M. McNally (1944–2020)
Michael H. Levin (1944–2024)
Karl W. Carter Jr. (1944–)
Maurice Le Gardeur (1944–)
J. Michael Walls (1944–)
Warren Woessner (1944–)
Norman Caplan (1945–1995)

Donald H. Vish (1945–2023)
Tomas Gayton (1945–2024)
Richard Alan Bunch (1945–)
Greg McBride (1945–)
James McKenna (1945–)
Chester S. Weinerman
  (1946–1990)
Steven Cahill (1946–1997)
Richard Krech (1946–2018)
G. Michael Loveall (1946–2022)
Nelson G. Alston (1946–)
Gary Jeshel Forrester (1946–)
Coyt Randal Johnston
  (1946–)
Susan Prospere (1946–)
Robert Lynch (1947–1989)
Kathleen Bogan (1947–2000)
Herbert Joseph Ludwig
  (1947–2005)
Samuel H. Weissbard
  (1947–2006)
Michael McPherson
  (1947–2008)
Adrian Oktenberg (1947–2014)
Wallace McCall (1947–2023)
Gregory Dyer Curtis
  (1947–2024)
Joseph Caldwell (1947–)

William L. Manchee (1947–)
Thomas H. Oehmke (1947–)
Steve Russell (1947–)
Ron Self (1947–)
Robert Whitehill (1947–)
Alfred–Maurice de Zayas
  (1947–)
David Bristol (1948–1993)
Thomas Soybel (1948–2010)
Helen M. Bailey (1948–)
Mel Belin (1948–)
Lawrence Joseph (1948–)
Mary Leader (1948–)
John R. O'Malley (1948–)
Manning Gilbert Warren III
  (1948–)
Charles Williams (1948–)
Mary Cynthia Dunlap
  (1949–2003)
Carl Russo (1949–2012)
D. Beecher Smith (1949–2024)
Lee Wm. Atkinson (1949–)
Bethami Auerbach (1949–)
Anthony Bernini (1949–)
Michael Blumenthal (1949–)
Jim Boyer (1949–)
Silvia Antonia Brandon–Perez
  (1949–)

A note about the compilation of the chronological indexes: Poets who were, for the briefest time associated with law, and lawyers who, by historical sources were identified as poets, have been included in the index. Some poets included for the index studied law and made little or no headway in the practice of law. Lawyers known for poetry published in newspapers and magazines have been included. *A further note*: Dates of deaths of some poets were established using Perplexity AI.

JAMES R. ELKINS was a longtime member of the law faculty at West Virginia University where he taught Criminal Law, Law and Psychiatry, and courses on Lawyers and Literature, Lawyers and Film, and Psychology for Lawyers. For more than two decades he served as editor of the *Legal Studies Forum*, a "legal studies" journal founded in the 1970s to promote critical, humanistic, interdisciplinary perspectives in the study of law.

Professor Elkins was awarded a University Benedum Distinguished Scholar Award for his interdisciplinary work. The award cites Professor Elkins for "[h]is writings on legal ethics, the professionalization of law students, women and the law, and narrative jurisprudence. [His writings are drawn] from a wide range of disciplines and are remarkably creative, original and insightful."

Elkins was born and grew up on a farm in western Kentucky and obtained his undergraduate and law degree from the University of Kentucky. After serving as a trial attorney with the Department of Justice, and as an Assistant U.S. Attorney in New Jersey, he obtained an LL.M. (Masters of Law) from Yale. His first teaching appointment was at DePaul University; he had visiting appointments at Washington & Lee, University of Kentucky, and the University of Massachusetts Amherst.

www.ingramcontent.com/pod-product-compliance
Lightning Source LLC
LaVergne TN
LVHW041337080426
835512LV00006B/496